Swindles, Stickups, and Robberies

Swindles, Stickups, and Robberies

Crimes that Shocked the World

Sean P. Steele

Grange
BOOKS

A FRIEDMAN GROUP BOOK
Published by Grange Books PLC
The Grange
Grange Yard
London SE1 3AG

ISBN 1-85627-706-2

SWINDLES, STICKUPS, AND ROBBERIES
Crimes that Shocked the World
was prepared and produced by
Michael Friedman Publishing Group, Inc.
15 West 26th Street
New York, NY 10010

Project Editor: Elizabeth Viscott Sullivan
Editor: Dana Rosen
Art Director: Jeff Batzli
Designer: Susan E. Livingston
Layout: Tanya Ross-Hughes
Photography Editor: Wendy Missan

Colour separations by Benday Scancolour Co. Ltd.
Printed in China by Leefung-Asco Printers Ltd.

Dedication

For Butch, The Great Boomer,
The Mick, Toughy, and The Duchess.

Acknowledgments

With thanks to Maryanne Melloan, Liz Sullivan, The Leonardo Group, *Perry Mason Loses*,
and the network of friends from New York to Austin to L.A.

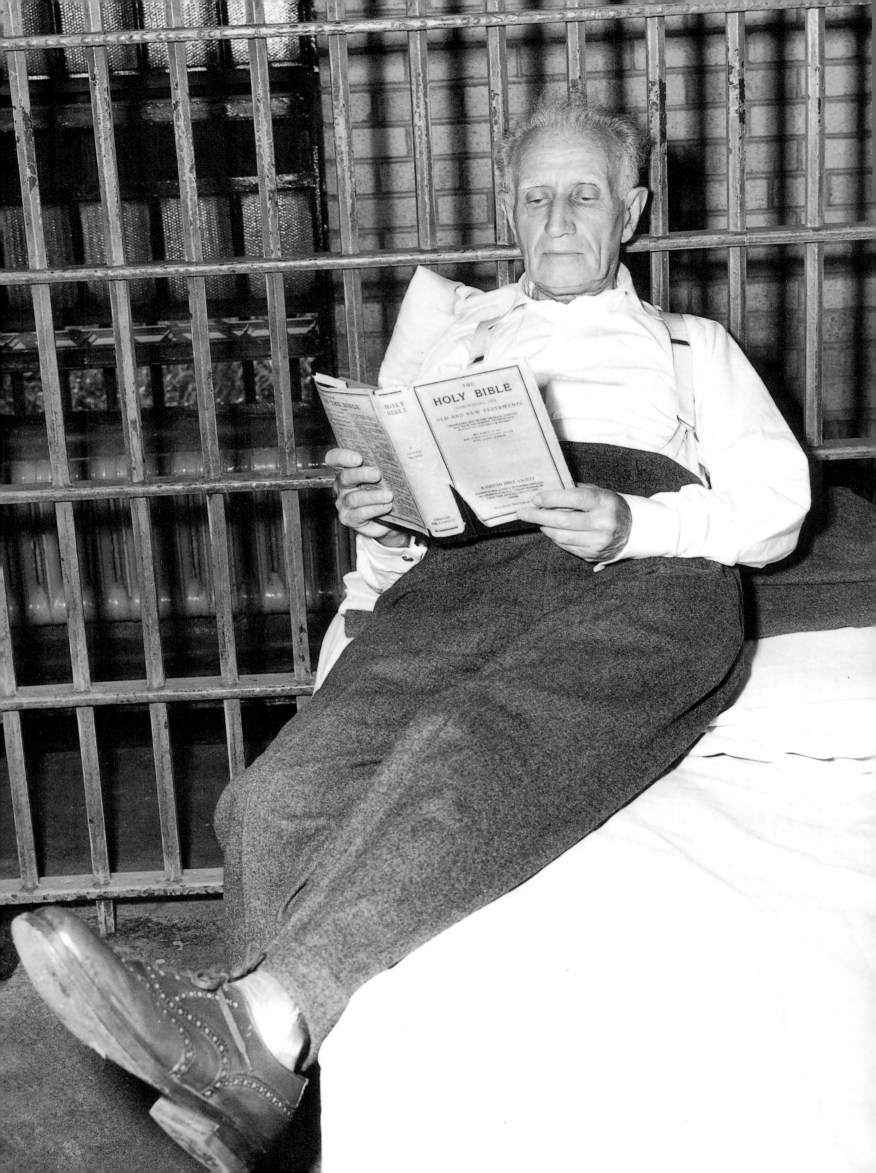

CONTENTS

INTROD

The earliest literature of western civilization heroically recounts the escapades of a great robber. The work is a Greek poem about a man who sacks cities and takes lives, not to raise or destroy democracy and not to enforce the word of his god on infidels—not at all. The man does these things just to take stuff that isn't his. The poem is Homer's *The Odyssey*; the man is Ulysses—Kirk Douglas played him in the movie.

Thieves and thievery remained a regular part of the landscape throughout history. One need only see the fortresses and walled villages of the Dark and Middle Ages to get a clue to how life was in the days after the fall of the Roman Empire: if you had anything worth taking, you lived behind high walls with a few hired soldiers. If you didn't have anything worth taking, you were generally exploited by those who did.

Brigandage was a widespread activity that recognized no class distinctions. All the way up through the time of Charles Dickens (1812–1870) in England, the world was a wild place. In jolly old(e) England, aristocratic "gentlemen" might join one of two violent society clubs of the day, either the Mohocks or the Bold Bucks. The Mohocks plundered and killed randomly just for a good rush, while the Bold Bucks added sexual depravation to the mix in order to liven

UCTION

up their sometimes dreary lives. It was a hard world for everyone, and children were not spared. "Childstrippers" would steal every stitch of clothing off a child's back to sell at market—probably to victims of other childstrippers. In this context, it is no surprise that highwaymen, thieves, and renegades like Robin Hood were the heroes of the day.

In the nineteenth century, when civilization tried to become more civilized, serfdom fell by the wayside, and citizens began to expect a safe world in which to live their lives and conduct their businesses. Police forces sprung up, cities no longer needed walls, and the public grew accustomed to a world where they had better than a fifty-fifty chance of getting from one place to another without molestation. Indeed, the world had become safer—although robbers and plunderers did not exactly vanish. After all, nothing is totally safe from those who prefer larceny to labor, pillage to plain life, and high risk to security.

Whether locked in a safe tucked inside an electronically monitored vault, or under the bed, or in transit, *anything* is vulnerable to those willing to risk everything to obtain it. And if force, skill, and planning do not suffice to separate a victim and his money, there is always the swindle. Here, then, within the pages of this volume, are accounts of the best who endeavor in pursuits of the worst kind.

Chapter

WHERE THE MONEY IS: BANKS

One

The banks and bankers of today evolved from the money changers and money-lenders of antiquity. Centuries ago, the spreading network of commerce among the emergent empires such as Persia, Greece, and Rome was aided in its development by the money changers, who dealt in different currencies and in gold bullion to mediate international business transactions. Since gold and other valuables accumulated in these early places of business and thieves were a concern of these proto-bankers, they conducted business in temples. The moneymen relied on superstition—they believed that the fear of angering Jupiter, Zeus, Yahweh, or whoever the local god might be would deter thieves. The system worked well, and it was rare that someone would make off with a moneylender's bags of drachma, denarii, or shekels.

By the Middle Ages, the moneylenders operated out of their own establishments, often seated behind benchlike tables called *bancums*. Bankers no longer relied on superstition to keep robbers away, just a few guards and the knowledge that it would be difficult for anyone to escape after robbing a building nestled in the middle of a densely populated city. The bankers knew that robbers had easier pickings raiding remote manors or waylaying wealthy travelers in the wilderness. Banks remained relatively safe for centuries.

Bank robbery, where the armed robber confronts the banker and demands money, emerged as a crime in the New World, far from the cities of old-world Europe and the shores of the Mediterranean Sea. In the small towns of America and Australia, banks did not have the security of a large surrounding populace. The New World also offered thousands of square miles of wilderness in which to hide once the robber cleared the town. It was a very different situation.

In the United States, the stick-'em-up style of robbery burgeoned during the Civil War as a means of raising money for military operations. Raiders on horseback from either the Union or the Confederacy would rob the bank of whatever opposing town they happened to be terrorizing at the moment, and the robbery was considered a legitimate act of war. When the war ended, however, out-of-work marauders, particularly those living in the West, wasted little time before resuming their wartime occupations with motives substantially less altruistic than patriotism.

The James-Younger Gang, a band of former Confederates headed by brothers Frank and Jesse, set the standard for the postwar boom in bank robbery. Other gangs formed when they saw—or perhaps remembered—how easy it was to knock over a bank. The plan was simple: storm a bank, wave guns around, yell "stick 'em up," and threaten to kill anyone within earshot; once the locals were sufficiently terrorized, ransack the teller drawers and the safe if it could be opened, and then

Fifteenth-century Europe: Medieval gentlemen with swords deposited their gold in banks that were for the most part secure.

ride out fast. It was a safe bet in those early days that no citizen would risk his or her life to stop the robbery, so all that remained to do was divvy up the loot.

"Get Your Guns, Boys! They're Robbing the Bank!"

The most spectacular robberies of the nineteenth century were both eventually bloody failures. The James-Younger Gang was reduced to simply the James Gang when the Youngers were all killed or captured at Northfield, Minnesota, on September 7, 1876. The James brothers made good their escape but decided never to hit another bank.

In 1892, the Dalton brothers gave a lesson in the dangers of envy. Wanting to eclipse the James brothers in the hearts and minds of the West, Bob, Grat, and young Emmet Dalton planned a double robbery of two banks in the center of Cof-

feyville, Kansas. On October 5, the Daltons and two henchmen rode into Coffeyville armed. Unfortunately, the citizens of that town were also armed to the teeth, and they fiercely resisted the Daltons with a hail of hot lead. Bob and Grat Dalton fell dead, and Emmet was captured after being wounded many times.

As robbers, the Daltons surpassed the James brothers only in the scale of their failure and the bloodiness of their demise. Emmet, however, may have exceeded Jesse James in compassion. Emmet was wounded when he rode back to the scene of the crime to carry off his fallen brother Bob. Jesse James' career was ended in quite a different fashion. While riding away from his last robbery in Northfield in 1876, Jesse James suggested finishing off his partners, the wounded Younger brothers, in order to aid in his own escape. Understandably vigorous objections from the Youngers and from Frank James persuaded Jesse to merely abandon his former partners rather than kill them. Not

Nineteenth-century America. Frontier ruffians with guns withdrew the gold of decent citizens from banks that were easy pickings.

surprisingly, Jesse was eventually shot in the back by one of his own men, while Emmet survived to go to jail.

In view of the consistently grim fate that ultimately faced most bank robbers, one might have thought that most prospective stickup men would have been deterred from pursuing such a dead-end career. History, of course, has proved just the opposite to be true. Bank robbery as a criminal endeavor has steadily boomed over the years.

A New Century

The ease of the stickup proved a great lure to the violent and malcontent, despite the solid police record for eventually capturing most outlaws. The turn of the twentieth century found old habits dying hard as Butch Cassidy and the Sundance Kid robbed the First National Bank of Winnemucca, Nevada, on September 19, 1900.

Horses gave way to automobiles and six-guns were replaced by automatics, but the basic pattern of the outlaw roaring in from the wilderness to strike at the town bank remained the same. Yet, even though the technique was the same, there was a difference in attitude. The twentieth-century bank robber was much more fatalistic than his brethren of the Old West, and knew the long-term odds were grim.

"Dear Sir. While I still have breath in my lungs, I will tell you what a dandy car you make. I have drove Fords exclusively when I could get away with one," wrote Clyde Barrow. In this letter to Henry Ford praising the Ford V-8, the romantic fatalism of the bank robber appears merely as an allusion. Bonnie Parker's poem (see opposite page), while less than Homeric, also alludes to the tragic destiny of the robber. Bonnie and Clyde did indeed "go down together" in a Ford V-8 that was riddled by 167 bullets in twelve seconds. Their biggest haul was worth a mere fifteen hundred dollars.

They're not sleeping. Bill Powers, Bob Dalton, Grat Dalton, and Dick Broadwell give silent, effective testimony to the wages of sin and bad planning after the Coffeyville debacle.

Bonnie Parker (pictured) and Clyde Barrow achieved their notoriety more for the nature of their bloody getaways than the size of their hauls.

Gunning and Running

On a November day in 1933, a well-dressed man walked into the American Bank and Trust Company of Racine, Wisconsin, with a Red Cross poster under his arm. When he tacked the poster over a window that allowed tellers to see the street from their cages, the tellers thought little of it. However, they were forced to take notice when John Dillinger strode in with two other men holding guns and announced that it was a robbery. The poster cleverly blocked anyone outside from seeing what was happening inside the bank. One teller resisted and was shot down on the spot, but not before he pushed an

WANTED

LESTER M. GILLIS,

aliases GEORGE NELSON, "BABY FACE" NELSON, ALEX GILLIS, LESTER GILES,
"BIG GEORGE" NELSON, "JIMMIE", "JIMMY" WILLIAMS .

On June 23, 1934, HOMER S. CUMMINGS, Attorney General of the United States, under the authority vested in him by an Act of Congress approved June 6, 1934, offered a reward of

$5,000.00

for the capture of Lester M. Gillis or a reward of

$2,500.00

for information leading to the arrest of Lester M. Gillis.

Age, 25 years; Heigh
133 pounds; Build, m
slate; Hair, light c
pation, oiler.

All claims to any of the aforesaid rew
as among claimants to the foregoing rewar
his decisions shall be final and conclusi
portions of any of said rewards as betwee
wards shall be paid to any official or em

If you are in possession of any inform
communicate immediately by telephone or t
sion of Investigation, United States Depa
forth on the reverse side of this notice.

The apprehension of Lester M. Gillis i
Agent W. C. Baum of the Division of Inves
1934.

June 25, 1934

TOP: *Of all his aliases, Lester Gillis preferred the moniker "Big George" Nelson. Gillis, thrown out of Al Capone's gang because he was too violent, hated the name "Baby Face," and few men addressed him as such.*

alarm that silently alerted the police station. Dillinger went into the vault to get at the real money, the cash reserves.

Outside, the trigger-happy George "Baby Face" Nelson kept an eye on things while hiding a rifle under his overcoat. He stayed calm when two cops strolled serenely past him and into the bank. The cops, checking out the alarm but sure that it was a mistake, entered the bank without even drawing their weapons.

Inside the bank, the policemen were taken by surprise—one was quickly dis-

Say It Ain't So

In addition to being a famous thief, John Dillinger had an unusual reputation for another reason as well, the result of a photograph (below) taken of him after he had been killed. In the photo, an arm stiffened by rigor mortis has raised the sheet covering Dillinger's body, giving the appearance that the deceased was a very well endowed villain. The photo was retouched by newspapers to eliminate the illusion, but the legend has remained.

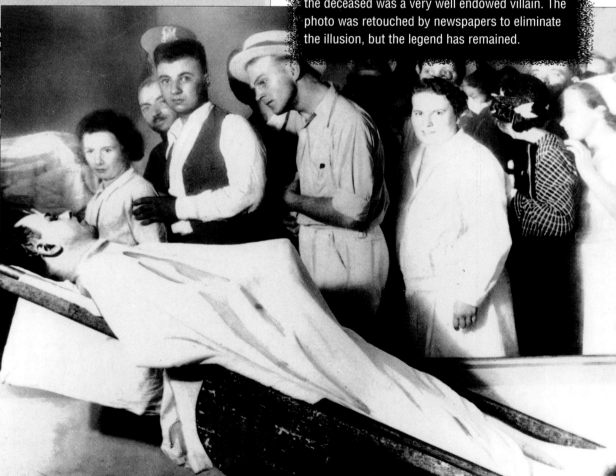

armed, and the second was shot when he resisted. Dillinger emerged from the vault and ordered his men and two hostages to leave the building. In the sunlight, Nelson brandished his rifle and fired at the onlookers who were trying to figure out what had transpired. Dillinger ordered his men into the getaway car and directed the hostages to ride on the outside running boards, for he was confident the police would hesitate to shoot at a car with a man and woman so exposed. The gang roared out of town and away from pursuit to the safety of the country. Once clear of the city and the law, Dillinger released his hostages.

The Racine job is a classic example of a 1930s robbery. The man who hung the Red Cross poster was veteran crook Harry "Pete" Pierpont, who had essentially been a professor in residence at the Indiana State Penitentiary. Pierpont taught Dillinger how to rob banks in prison, which is where a lot of small-time troublemakers gained the know-how to graduate to big-time crime.

Frank "Jelly" Nash was another prison teacher, who tutored Kate "Ma" Barker's boys in the finer art of theft. When Nash left jail, he joined the nascent Barker Gang and was present when they hit the Cloud County Bank at Concordia, Kansas, for $240,000 in bonds and cash. The gang later hit the National Bank in Fairbury,

Bank Robber as Public Servant

"My conscience doesn't hurt me. I stole from the banks, they stole from the people. All we did was help raise insurance rates."

Harry Pierpoint, henchman for John Dillinger

Harry Pierpoint was the early leader of what later became the Dillinger Gang and engineered the bold robberies of two Indiana police stations to acquire guns and bulletproof vests.

The felonious Barker Boys. Dock Barker (left), the most violent of the Barker Gang, began his last prison stint for kidnapping in 1935. He died trying to escape from Alcatraz four years later.

Ma Barker's Bloody Brood's Bloody Rampage

Location	Crime(s)	Barker Involved
West Plains, Missouri	Robbed store/Killed sheriff	Fred
Mountain View, Missouri	Robbed bank	Fred
Minneapolis, Minnesota	Robbed bank	Fred
St. Paul, Minnesota	Kidnapped William Hamm	Dock (Ma's plan)
Chicago, Illinois	Robbed Federal Reserve truck/Killed policeman	Dock
Beloit, Wisconsin	Robbed bank	Fred
Wahpeton, North Dakota	Robbed bank	Fred
Concordia, Kansas	Robbed bank	Fred (Ma's plan)
Bixby, Oklahoma	Robbed bank	Fred
Minneapolis, Minnesota	Kidnapped Campbell's Soup heir	Dock (Ma's plan)
Lake Weir, Florida	Died by machine gun	Ma and Fred

Nebraska, for $151,350—loot a hundred times greater than any haul raked in by Bonnie and Clyde.

Nash was later captured and accidentally killed in a storm of machine-gun fire loosed by Charles "Pretty Boy" Floyd and accomplices who were trying to free him, an event termed the Kansas City Massacre of June 17, 1933. Nash died along with four lawmen, and the massacre was instrumental in turning public opinion against robbers and bolstering support for the FBI. The Barkers went on to kidnap and ransom the Hamm's Brewery heir for $100,000 as they cut a $3.5 million swath across America, before Ma Barker was killed in a bloody Florida shoot-out.

Although this running and gunning was great stuff for newspaper reporters, movie moguls, and a thrilled public, it had little allure for the professional thief, who looks upon his occupation as both a life-long and long-life endeavor. The professional thief, who would soon dominate the crime scene, preferred to minimize the spilling of blood, taking particular care about his own.

Fred Barker (left) died with his mother, Kate "Ma" Barker, in a bloody shoot-out at a Lake Weir, Florida, house (below). Some say the FBI invented Ma Barker's reputation as the brains of the outfit to justify machine-gunning an old woman.

The Actor

A more sophisticated technique for robbing banks was perfected by Willie Sutton, the single most prolific bank robber of all time. Sutton grew up in Irish Brooklyn, New York, and was a tough city kid all the way. From his earliest days, Sutton was a thief, and as an adult, he found ways to rob urban banks by turning the ever-present hustling crowds to his advantage. Sutton also provided the history of bank robbery with its brightest quote; it was Sutton who answered the question, "Why do you rob banks?" with the characteristically direct answer, "Because that's where the money is."

Sutton's trademark as a robber was the inventive use of disguises to gain access to banks before they opened their doors for business. The bank's morning guard or porter would unknowingly open the locked doors for the wiry, smiling deliveryman who rapped on the glass. Before he knew it, the guard had the package in one hand and a book for signing in the other, as the deliveryman kept up a pleasant chatter. With his hands occupied, the guard could do nothing when Sutton pulled out his own pistol and took command of the room. As the years passed, this clever technique gained Sutton the nickname Willie the Actor.

A classic Sutton scheme was the Corn Exchange Bank robbery of 1931 in New York City. Sutton spent weeks observing the routines of the bank's employees as they prepared for opening every day. From these observations Sutton learned when they arrived, in what order they arrived, and their designated tasks. Near the bank on 110th Street between Broadway and Amsterdam Boulevard was a subway station that provided plenty of pedestrian activity as busy New Yorkers hurried to work. When Sutton and his colleagues were certain that they had observed enough, they made their move.

Sutton chose a policeman's uniform for disguise on that particular morning and approached the bank from the subway kiosk after waving nonchalantly to a real cop stationed just a block away. Sutton tapped on the bank door with his police baton to get the attention of the porter, who was the only person in the bank at that hour. The porter let Sutton in without question and the robbery began. As always, Sutton took charge at gunpoint, establishing his authority with a voice that was confident and decisive yet also reassuring. His manner made victims feel that they would come out unharmed as long as they cooperated.

Sutton first ordered the porter to let his partner inside, and the two criminals took each employee captive as he or she came in for work. Sutton could talk a good line and even had some of the female tellers chatting about their love lives as he waited for the bank manager to arrive, for Sutton knew that the bosses always arrived last and a little late. The manager was needed to get into the vault; he had the combination and whatever keys might be necessary. Once the manager was in hand, Sutton secured his cooperation by making it clear that there was no other choice and that by not resisting he was looking after the safety of his workers. Sutton never used bullying language or humiliating techniques. His ego soothed, the manager opened the vault, and Sutton helped himself to thirty thousand dollars.

After giving his partner a head start, Sutton left the employees in a conference

"The Actor," Willie Sutton, who gave bank robbery its greatest line, is shown against two of his favorite disguises—cop and deliveryman. Sutton was as good at breaking out of jail as he was at getting into banks; he twice escaped from maximum-security prisons.

room and calmly left the bank. The alarm immediately went off and the real cop down the street raced right past Sutton, who was still in uniform, to get to the bank. Sutton was able to vanish into the crowds of city people who were too busy to think twice about another seemingly unremarkable cop in the subway.

Sutton used the same modus operandi in more than a hundred robberies and was a popular public figure because no one was hurt in any of his jobs. Although the wily robber was a genius at confounding the police, he was not as successful at combatting the betrayal of his various partners, and he did three stints in prison. In a career spanning decades, Sutton stole an estimated two million dollars and was last released from prison in 1969 to become a security consultant. He died a free man in 1980; however, his techniques lived on.

The Big Tucson Robbery

Borrowing a page or two from Willie Sutton's book, two robbers set themselves up outside a small branch of the First National Bank of Arizona in Tucson in a van that was disguised to look as though it belonged to the telephone company. It was a pretty spring morning in 1981 before business hours had begun, and the robbers used their disguises to get the drop on the morning porter and two top managers as they appeared for work.

The porter, the bank manager, and the operations manager were taken at gunpoint and told that their families would be harmed if they did not cooperate. Each manager knew half the combination to the vault, and they opened the steel door for the two robbers. From this tiny bank with only four teller windows, the robbers made off with $3.3 million in cash; they were aware that the tiny bank was the depository that all the local branches of the First National used to hold their cash surpluses. The whole operation was over in twenty minutes; the thieves were never caught. Wherever they are today, the thieves are living on the largest amount of cash ever taken from a bank at gunpoint.

Bank Burglary: The Biggest Bank Jobs

Despite the color and dash of gun-wielding bank robbers, the biggest bank jobs in history have been pulled off by bank burglars. For robbers, the obstacles are guards, witnesses, and possibly the police. For bank burglars the main problem is the vault, with its steel door and thick walls designed to be impervious to thieves.

Although such work takes time, special tools, and often explosives, it offers a richer payoff when the job is successful. Over the years, bank burglary has emerged as the most elevated and lucrative form of bank robbery. A thief who can stealthily penetrate alarm systems and thick vault walls can pillage the safes and deposit boxes within at leisure. Instead of the few fleeting minutes allowed an armed robber to snatch up whatever he can and flee, the burglar can set up shop for hours—or even days—and do a proper job of pillage.

The defenses guarding the treasures of a modern bank generally consist of a layered system of electronic surveillance, steel, and concrete. Defeating these defenses takes a combination of skill, nerve, meticulousness, and hard, dirty work. The biggest bank job in American history is a study in the art of the master thief.

The Great American Bank Job

To a professional's eye, the modest-looking Laguna Niguel branch of the United Bank of California was perched on a cliff overlooking the Pacific Ocean like a great, fattened bird. South of Los Angeles and swollen with the riches of wealthy Orange County, this Laguna Niguel bank was the center point of a newly constructed shopping strip. On a February day in 1972, Amil Dinisio stopped in the fine weather to take his first good look at the bank. It was his trained eye that noticed how a little access road that ran behind the bank could not be seen either from the highway far below at the foot of the cliff or from the parking lot of the shopping center. He noted that many of the bank's customers were elderly: often careful with their money, the elderly have a tendency to store their valuables in safe-deposit boxes. Dinisio had flown to sunny California to find just such a bank, and now his planning could begin.

As the compact man with average looks boarded the jet back to Ohio, the stewardess could not have known that Mr. Dinisio was a master thief. There was certainly nothing memorable about his manner or his looks, and such anonymity is key to the best of thieves. Loyalty is also critical, and once he got to Ohio, Dinisio carefully gathered together a gang to break into the California bank. All known members of the gang, with a single exception, were related by blood or marriage to Dinisio. Precautions like this had kept authorities from securing a conviction against Dinisio even though he was believed to have been involved in a dozen bank jobs which had lightened a dozen midwestern banks of thirty million dollars. It was probably his local notoriety that made Dinisio look west.

The gang was composed of six to eight men, all from Ohio. In late February they flew out to California, many on the same plane, and made arrangements to rent a townhouse located a few miles from the bank. One member began gathering the necessary tools: drills, saws, special hammers, exhaust fans, and gas masks. An observation point that was higher and further inland than the bank was found so that one of them could keep a constant watch on the bank and note everything that went on during an average day without being noticed. These meticulous preparations and observations took weeks.

In the small shopping center next door to the bank was a pharmacy that stayed open seven days a week. Because people in the pharmacy would be just a few feet from the bank vault and might be able to hear loud noises, work could be done only at night after the pharmacy closed. Secondary concerns were a bar across the parking lot from the bank that stayed open late into the night and the on-site security guard hired to keep an eye on the unfinished shopping center. The guard operated out of a trailer in the parking lot. Confident that these problems could be overcome, Dinisio was ready for the first phase of the assault.

Casing

Despite all the observations from outside the bank and the few forays he made inside during business hours under the pretense of having to change a big bill, Dinisio was still unable to decide whether he could successfully do the job. He needed to take a closer look.

One night a car cruised through the quiet parking lot and slipped down the access road, out of sight behind the bank. The car left Dinisio and a helper behind equipped with a ladder, power tools, electrical wire, and a bucket of tar. Dinisio led the way up the ladder to the roof, where he found the first necessity for the operation—a 220-volt power line running to the air conditioner, which could be tapped to allow them to run the tools.

As his lookouts, who were posted all around, kept an eye out for any interference, Dinisio wired his drill and saw into the power line and cut a neat hole in the flat roof of the bank. After carefully reaching down to pull up a few ceiling tiles below, Dinisio lowered the ladder (itself stolen from a nearby church) into the gloomy bank lobby. Inside the lobby,

Infamy. The feared Clyde Barrow (right) leans on his beloved Ford V-8, which he liked to keep loaded with weaponry. Police found four Browning automatic rifles, a shotgun, nine assorted pistols, fifteen license plates, and a saxophone secreted in the car in which he and Bonnie died. Bill Dalton (above) and Emmet Dalton (opposite, top left) who were both shot to pieces in Coffeyville, Kansas (Bill fatally), were cousins of Jim Younger (opposite, bottom), who was shot to pieces and captured after the Northfield, Minnesota, raid.

ABOVE: *No biz like show biz. Cole Younger, captured after the Northfield fiasco, was paroled and pardoned at the turn of the century. He went on to found a marginally successful Wild West show with Frank James.*

Dinisio shone his light first on the vault door to be sure it was a brand he was familiar with—it was. Next, the telephone box in the rear of the lobby came under the thief's scrutiny. The sensors in the vault that would register any movement or vibration inside were wired to this box, where they were connected via direct telephone lines to the nearest police station. This system was also familiar to Dinisio, and he knew he could probably disarm it when the time came. He could do the job.

After scaling the ladder back to the top of the building, Dinisio and his companion carefully replaced the ceiling tiles and then the section they had cut from the roof. Tar was brushed over the fresh cuts so that no trace of this preliminary break-in would remain.

For the next week, business went on as usual in the bank as the gang of thieves prepared for their final assault. On the night of March 24, 1972, Dinisio and his team arrived at the rear of the bank. Because it was Friday, the men would have the entire weekend to work, and they would use all three nights of it. The bank's defenses would be attacked and disarmed in succession.

The Alarm Systems

First, there was the standard bell alarm mounted high on the rear wall of the building. The loud bell housed in the vented metal box was wired to the vault and designed to raise a clamor should anyone tamper with the vault or the alarm box itself. The ladder was raised, and one of the thieves scampered up the rungs with an aerosol container. When he shoved the nozzle into one of the louvers, the bell came to life, but the two elements being sprayed into the box from the aerosol can rendered it useless. Cold Freon froze the bell so that the only sound was a dull thudding; even that ceased quickly as soon as polyurethane foam filled the box, hardened, and rendered the clapper unable to move. In just a few seconds, the sound emanating from the box of hardening plastic was reduced to the faint humming of the little bell motor, which was inaudible above the breeze.

The next obstacles were the vault sensors that ran to the telephone lines. Dinisio climbed onto the roof and entered the bank through the hole he had made days before. This time Dinisio brought some electronic gear to the phone box toward the rear of the dark lobby area. Until the vault sensor alarms were verifiably defeated, there was no reason to proceed. These vault sensors sent a steady current through a telephone line leading to the nearest police station. Any vibration in the vault would cause the sensor to disrupt the steady current, and this would trigger the police alarms and bring a flood of cops onto the scene. After getting inside the telephone box, Dinisio identified the alarm wires among the regular telephone connections. He connected the lines for the police station alarms to a steady current transmitter that he had brought with him. Next, Dinisio cut the lines leading from the telephone box back to the vault, thus disconnecting the sensors and replacing their signal with one from the transmitter. If done correctly, it would not matter if the vault sensors were disrupted, for there would still be a steady current over the line and no alarm would be set off. The only way to know if the sensors were properly disconnected, however, was to wait and see if the police responded.

Done with this task, Dinisio flew up the ladder and then back down to the embankment behind the bank. He listened intently with the other men to a police radio they had brought. Nothing. They waited half an hour to be sure there was no response, then began the next phase of the operation.

The Vault

With the electronic safeguards out of the way, next came the physically taxing work of penetrating the vault. The walls and ceiling of the bank vault were eighteen inches (45.7cm) thick, made of tough concrete reinforced by a grid of steel rods crisscrossed every twelve inches (30.4cm) within the walls. While several gang members loaded dirt into large burlap sacks outside on the embankment, several other men sweated and cursed over drills in the crawl space above the vault ceiling. Dinisio chose to attack the ceiling for two reasons: first, the ceiling is sometimes not as thick as the vault walls; second, if anyone were to look into the bank, they would be unable to detect any trace of the work that was going on inside. For hours, the men wrestled the heavy bags of dirt up the ladder or leaned into masonry drills carving out holes only an inch (2.5cm) deep in the vault's ceiling.

After the holes were drilled and eighteen bags of dirt were in place, a new expert came to the fore: a demolition man. He packed the holes with high explosives and carefully fused them to a single detonating device. A dozen of the bags of dirt were laid atop the charges to force the blast downward; the rest of the bags were piled atop one another to make a shield for the explosives expert and his detona-

tor. Everyone but the explosives man was ordered out of the building and down to the embankment.

Outside, Dinisio and the other men crouched around the police radio to wait and see if there would be any response to the explosion. BOOM! As soon as they heard the sound of the blast, the thieves looked nervously at one another and fought down panic. Surely everyone in Southern California had heard that. Dinisio stayed cool. From the police radio came nothing but silence. There was no reaction from the night around them either—the security guard did not stir from his trailer. No one else was listening with the same level of nervous anticipation as the thieves. Dinisio led his crew back up the ladder and onto the roof.

Acrid smoke and dust belched from the hole. Someone called to the explosives expert as the rest put on gas masks and set up an exhaust fan to suck out the unbreathable air. They called again to the explosives expert. Deafened by the blast, the expert did not respond at first, but otherwise he was all right. Dinisio dropped into the hole and went to the blast site.

The weight of the dirt had done the trick, and the blast had punctured a hole in the concrete top of the vault. Steel rods still crisscrossed the three-foot (91.4cm) opening, but they could take care of those the second night. With dawn coming soon, the thieves worked only on clearing out the smoke and then patching up the hole in the roof before leaving. It had been a good start.

During daylight, the members of the gang other than those charged with watching the scene rested. Business went on as usual in the shopping center all around the closed bank. The only signs

Felonious (but True) Facts

• Bonnie Parker, notorious bank robber and murderess, was concerned that false accounts of her smoking cigars would make her seem unfeminine.

• John Dillinger's brain was stolen after his autopsy.

• There is strong evidence that Butch Cassidy did not die in South America but returned and lived a quiet life well into the 1930s.

• When Willie Sutton was last arrested, the police found seven thousand dollars hidden in his room. Sutton commented, "It's never safe in a bank."

• Los Angeles, California, averages more than four bank robberies *per day*. The extensive highway system is great for getaways.

TOP: *Willie Sutton (bottom, center) lost public sympathy when it was alleged that he gunned down a potential witness against him. Sutton convincingly denied the charge, but his last prison sentence was a harsh thirty-to-life for handgun possession.*

OPPOSITE: *Now they got him. John Dillinger stands to face the music in 1934 in Tucson, Arizona, where he was accused of killing a police officer. The world expected that Dillinger would be put away for good.*

BOTTOM, RIGHT: *Now they don't. Months after the Tucson arraignment, Dillinger escaped from the maximum-security prison at Crown Point, Indiana, and posed for this picture. The pistol in his left hand is the fake he used to bluff his way out of the gates of Crown Point.*

that anything was amiss—the fresh digging in the side of the embankment and a trickle of solidified plastic on the outer alarm box—went unnoticed. Night came again, leaving only the security guard and bar patrons in the area. Dinisio and company returned.

Immediately, the gang attacked the steel rods with torches and hammers. Many hours later, early on Sunday morning, the first thief dropped into the vault. It was still hard to see clearly in the dusty, smoky room, but the safe-deposit boxes were there waiting for them. The room quickly filled with the members of the gang. All wore cotton gloves now, which replaced the heavy leather ones they had been wearing for the other work. The gloved hands now held sledgehammers, which had one end tapered to a wedge. BAM! The first box was opened with one mighty stroke, the double locks no match for this weapon. Bonds, cash, and jewels poured out. BAM! BAM! More boxes, more loot. As in all burglaries, the gathering of the loot was the fun part, and discipline inside the vault began to break down. Pillaged boxes piled up on one side of the vault as the men worked feverishly at the task at hand. The paper valuables were neatly stacked in one spot, while the jewels and other precious items began to form a formidable pile in another.

Outside, daylight approached and the looting ceased because the hammering would surely be heard at the pharmacy next door. The thieves again left the scene. The last day passed tensely—they were so close. For most, sleeping was impossible; even sitting still was an ordeal. Evening at last approached, and the security guard at the shopping center made his usual cursory look around before retiring to his

trailer. As the day ended, the thieves' final night of work could begin.

That last night, the thieves' hammers opened 468 of the five hundred boxes, and the mass of the loot was impressive, filling several large bags. Dinisio had calculated correctly; this bank's large amount of older customers meant that many valuables were inside the safe-deposit boxes. Just a few hours before dawn, the burlap bags stuffed with cash, jewels, traveler's checks, and rare coins were passed down the ladders and into the cars. Shortly before sunrise, the cars were driven away. And by the time the sun rose over Laguna Niguel, the thieves were far away.

Final Precaution

To allow more time for getting away, the thieves had taken the usual precaution of welding the vault door shut to delay discovery. The bank opened as usual, but when an employee went to open the vault door, it appeared to be stuck. The bank employee called a locksmith, with no one suspecting that a robbery had occurred. After the locksmith tried everything he could to open the door, he explained at midafternoon that nothing would open it—they'd have to break in. He suggested that they go through the ceiling to avoid damaging the lobby and interrupting business. Only in the middle of the afternoon, when the locksmith saw the debris in the crawl space above the vault, was the break-in finally discovered.

The authorities found a crime scene devoid of any usable evidence. There were no prints, only a few bits of tools and cigarette butts, and little else. It looked as though whoever pulled off the job might get away with the biggest bank robbery in American history—five million dollars in jewels, cash, traveler's checks, and negotiable bonds.

Although they had acted perfectly at the crime scene, the Dinisio gang made a few errors elsewhere that proved fatal. The gang pulled a nearly identical job in Ohio a few months later that drew the attention of the FBI, who linked the two jobs. When the bureau checked transportation records, they found Dinisio's name and other known associates on a

gotten to turn on the washer, and the feds harvested fingerprints from every thief, including Dinisio. This evidence was enough for federal search warrants to be issued, which led to the discovery of most of the loot and the imprisonment of the thieves who had been so perfect inside the bank. Had Dinisio laid low, flown under an assumed name, and washed the dishes, he would most likely still be at large enjoying the largest haul in the history of the United States.

Other Notable American Robbers

Butch Cassidy Butch robbed both trains and banks. Especially adept at arranging for swift getaways, he would plot the route of his gang's flights and pre-position fresh horses along the way so that they could outrun any pursuit. He was reputedly killed in Colombia, where he had moved with the notorious Sundance Kid when a life of crime became too tough in the United States.

Ma Barker and Family Although elderly Ma Barker (who was a girl in Missouri when Jesse James was terrorizing the West) never took part in a crime herself, the FBI claimed she was the mastermind behind the Barker Gang's bloody career of bank robbery, kidnapping, and murder in the 1930s. Some argue that Barker was painted as a sinister character by the federal government to justify shooting the old woman to death with a machine gun in Florida.

Charles "Pretty Boy" Floyd An Oklahoma boy who ran with the Barkers and the Dillinger Gang during the Great Depression, Floyd despised his nickname, which he acquired as a youth and could not shake during his life of crime. Floyd was a Robin Hood–type and possessed a certain western charm that made him a folk hero in his home state.

Where are the Stetsons? Butch Cassidy (seated, right) specialized in planning escapes. Western robbers were called "long riders" because their only safety lay in staying in the saddle after a crime and vanishing into the vast American frontier. Cassidy is pictured with the rest of The Wild Bunch, including the Sundance Kid (seated, left).

single flight to California; the gang had not bothered to use assumed names. Furthermore, the townhouse near the bank that the gang used as a headquarters was leased to one of the members.

When the FBI went to the townhouse in hopes of proving the presence of the gang in California at the time of the crime, they initially found nothing; Dinisio's men had wiped everything clean before moving out. But as the agents were about to abandon the scene, someone checked the dishwasher and found a load of dishes inside. One of the gang members had for-

Charles Arthur Floyd abhorred the nickname "Pretty Boy," whose origin was either the police or a couple of prostitutes. Even so, Hollywood took the handle to heart and cast pretty boy actor Fabian Forte (4), rough and pretty Robert Conrad (1, extreme left by the moll), and homespun handsome Steve Kanaly (2) to portray Floyd (3), here photographed on what clearly was a bad hair day.

Who's the Prettiest "Pretty Boy" Floyd?

Robert Conrad
Young Dillinger
1964

Fabian Forte
A Bullet for Pretty Boy
1971

Steve Kanaly
Dillinger
1973

3999

Flattering Casting

Ma Barker	Shelley Winters as quasi–Ma Barker in *Bloody Mama* (1970)
John Dillinger	Robert Conrad as Dillinger in *The Lady in Red* (1979)
Jesse James	Tyrone Power in *Jesse James* (1939) **or** Robert Wagner in *The True Story of Jesse James* (1956)

"Pretty Boy" was not the only robber prettied up by Tinseltown. Matronly Kate "Ma" Barker (6) was clearly the inspiration for Bloody Mama, *whose title role featured onetime sexpot Shelly Winters (5). In* The Lady in Red, *Robert Conrad (7) met a bloody death as John Dillinger. Robert Wagner (8, far left), whose face is too handsome to be covered up even during a stickup, is but one of many to portray Jesse James. Wagner had a tough act to follow: megahandsome megastar Tyrone Power (9) had done a turn as Jesse twenty-seven years earlier.*

Dynamic Duos in Fact and Film

Bonnie and Clyde

Dorothy Provine and Jack Hogan
The Bonnie Parker Story (1958)

Faye Dunaway and Warren Beatty
Bonnie and Clyde (1967)

The public's lukewarm response to the Provine-Hogan version (1) of Bonnie and Clyde in the fifties led the powers that be in Hollywood to doubt the dramatic power of their story. Warren Beatty revived the whole gangster movie genre when he produced and starred in his own version teamed with Faye Dunaway (2). The genuine Texas articles (3) ham it up for the camera in a light moment between murders and robberies.

Frank and Jesse James pose with their mother (4), who lost an arm when some Pinkerton detectives bombed her house thinking her sons were holed up inside. It is believed that Kate Barker was acquainted with the James brothers in her childhood. Even Roy Rogers (5, left) got into the act of playing Jesse James. So did Tyrone Power, with Henry Fonda playing older brother Frank (7). Real-life brothers James and Stacy Keach played the roles during the brief period that westerns were revived in the early 1980s (6).

Jesse and Frank James

Tyrone Power and Henry Fonda
Jesse James (1939)

Roy Rogers and Michael Worth
Days of Jesse James (1939)

Jeffrey Hunter and Robert Wagner
The True Story of Jesse James (1956)

James and Stacy Keach
The Long Riders (1980)

The French Way: The World's Biggest Bank Robbery

"Sans armes, sans haine, et sans violence." It is a pretty good credo for a life: "Without guns, without hatred, and without violence." Some might even say it is admirable. But the president of the large Société Generale bank in Nice, France, was less than gratified to see the slogan scrawled on the wall inside his supposedly impenetrable vault, which had been sacked by thieves who had been able to make off with the biggest take in the history of bank robbery. Their leader proved to be one of the most colorful characters in the entire history of crime.

Albert Spaggiari is as different from Amil Dinisio as crêpes are from hamburgers. The romance-seeking Frenchman had been a paratrooper during the French chapter of the Vietnam War and had later devoted himself to right-wing causes. He preferred the action arms of these organizations and had once had Charles de Gaulle in the crosshairs of his rifle but had opted not to fire. Spaggiari did a turn in prison on charges of running an illegal press and having a cache of arms. When he emerged, it looked like he had gone straight, marrying a nurse and making a career of photography in Nice. But looks were deceiving.

Living snugly on the French Riviera, Spaggiari developed contacts with the political underground, which in Nice is pretty much the same milieu as the criminal underground. In the mid-1970s, Spaggiari concocted a plan for robbing the venerable Société Generale. He went to *Le Gang des Marseillais* (The Marseilles Mob) with his scheme to tunnel from a sewer

Where were you when they needed ya? A gang of gendarmes struggle to remove the tons of equipment abandoned by the gang who pulled off the biggest job ever in Nice.

line into the underground vault of the grand old bank. Impressed with the scheme, the mob helped Spaggiari spring a tunneling expert from prison in order to explore the plan's possibilities more carefully. The group sloshed through the sewer in high waders, and it may have been the rats or the stink or the darkness, but the mob ultimately said no to the project. The tunnel man, however, was impressed enough to stay aboard.

Spaggiari now had to recruit a gang from the freelance talent around Nice, and he wasted no time assembling some of the best and worst men in the area to attack the bank. With a gang formed, Spaggiari began assembling equipment. He parceled out purchases throughout the continent to avoid drawing attention and to avoid being traceable once the deed was done. By May 1976, they were ready to start.

The Mother of All Bank Jobs

May 1976. It was night in Nice in the sewer—where the light never reaches anyway—when the caper began. An electrical extension line snaked a hundred yards (91.4m) through the muck to power the lights that would be needed. The power line originated in a plug on city property before plunging into a sewer hole; it ended at the spot where tunneling was to begin. That night, three men started the grueling work in a space too low for anyone to stand, twenty-five feet (7.6m) away from the vault wall. They would have to work at night, when there would be no interruptions from real sewer workers; the only eyes upon them at night belonged to the rats.

As the digging progressed, buckets were filled with the muddy earth and emptied into a dead-end sewer a dozen yards away by hunched-over men dragging them in the confined space. The tunnel expert relieved the diggers periodically in order to cement the side walls and brace the ceiling from caving in. It was knuckle-busting, maddening work, and the two-by-three-foot (60.9 by 91.4cm) tunnel was completed after eight weeks—an average advance of less than six inches (15.2cm) a day.

July 16, 1976. Friday night. While a van was parked unobtrusively in front of the bank and a car was stationed to watch another nearby entrance to the sewer, the main assault team began its initial approach a few miles away—underground. Like many coastal cities, Nice lies where a river flows into the sea, but what is special about Nice is that its river runs through a channel located beneath the streets of the city right through the central network of Nice's storm sewers. In the summer, when the river's water is little more than a trickle, a broad road is exposed that runs beside the riverbed under Nice. On this particular night, a Land-Rover, packed with men and gear, followed the riverbank road down into the tunnel under the unsuspecting city.

The Land-Rover rumbled along the dark underground road to a junction with a sewer pipe four hundred yards (365.7m) from where the tunnel men had done their work. Since they could drive no further, the men piled out of the Land-Rover and began inflating rubber rafts and truck inner tubes, which they then tied together to form a caravan. Spaggiari directed the men as the first load of equipment was floated on the rafts for the trip up the sewer and away from the river.

While leading the nervous, crouched-over men through the dark, musty under-world, Spaggiari was quick with a joke or a pat on the shoulder to loosen them up as they covered the first few hundred yards toward the freshly dug tunnel. All the men wore high wader boots to keep off the water and the stink as they sloshed toward the intensifying glow of the tunnel work lights. The boats and inner tubes loaded with hammers, drills, and tanks trailed out behind the men like a sewer-going train, and this train would make several more trips in the next few hours to move the ton (0.9t) of equipment needed for the job.

Spaggiari smiled and shook hands with his tunnel expert before going in to inspect the narrow entrance that led from the sewer to the exposed vault wall. He was pleased to discover that the miners had already chipped out a six-inch (15.2cm) crater in the vault's twelve-inch (30.4cm) -thick wall. In practically every other bank in the world, vault sensors would have reacted to the vibrations and alerted the police. One of the advantages of hitting this bank, however, was that no vault sensors existed to alert the police that anything was amiss. The vault door was so thick, and the other walls considered so inaccessible, that the bank's insurer, Lloyd's of London, had agreed that no further precautions needed to be taken.

Spaggiari assigned teams of men to first drill and then hammer the rest of the way through the wall. An industrial-strength exhaust fan whirred to life to carry away the prodigious amounts of dust that would be generated by the drills and hammers. The drilling began with the expectation that they would have the work done before dawn on Saturday. For

hours the men, wearing goggles and heavy gloves, took turns crawling into the tunnel. When the holes were finally drilled, the men again took turns, this time each delivering thirty powerful hammer strokes to the wall.

Dawn came and went, but still the vault wall was not breached. Nerves frayed. Men cursed and bled and went on hammering. Spaggiari, distributing water, cigarettes, and one-liners to his men, supervised it all with unfailing spirit. By noon they had been hammering at the wall for twelve solid hours, yet the inner vault was still out of reach.

At last, at four o'clock on Saturday afternoon, a hammer smashed through the wall. A cheer went up, but it still took another five hours to make the hole big enough for a man to fit through. Before another cheer could be given voice, the lead man found a new obstacle—the hole was blocked by the back of a thirty-ton (27.2t) armored safe-deposit cabinet. Spaggiari ordered the lights doused in the sewer and radioed the van above in front of the bank. He got a quick reply.

The two men in the van pulled up to a manhole cover in the street in full view of the evening diners at a nearby cafe. One man set up an electric-company "Men at Work" sign and a flashing light, while the other pulled the manhole cover off with a pick. The first man quickly descended into the hole and received from his partner a hundred-pound (45.4kg) hydraulic lever, which was passed down to the thieves waiting in the dark sewer. The man crawled back out of the hole, the cover was replaced, and the sign was taken down. Twenty-six seconds was all the operation took before the van drove off again, and none of the dozen or so people

in the cafe would later be able to recall the face of either "electrical worker."

Underground, the lights flashed back to life, and the lever was manipulated into place near the hole in the vault wall. Anchored against a tunnel brace, the lever eased the thirty-ton (27.2t) cabinet out of the way. At two o'clock Sunday morning, Spaggiari entered the vault followed close behind by his men.

Tired, red-rimmed eyes followed the flashlight beam as it searched for the light switch in the vault. As soon as Spaggiari flipped on the lights, he assigned someone to weld the vault door shut—this room was now his fortress. One large man took a hacksaw and made short work of the portcullises that shielded the safe-deposit boxes and protected the night depository. Another man with a blowtorch began melting the hinges of the safe-deposit boxes. The treasures of the vault were now at their fingertips.

At first, the men worked with precision and control. With the vault door sealed, no one could surprise them, and a feeling of safety calmed their hands. Safe-deposit boxes began to yield to the blowtorches and crowbars. Cash, jewels, and bonds were released. The men exchanged glances and became giddy. The tension from weeks of preparation and the unbroken hours in the narrow tunnel erupted into an orgiastic explosion of joy and relief as the men went nuts, throwing cash and bonds into the air and laughing insanely.

Spaggiari let them rejoice for a while before breaking the spell with his raised voice. In the sudden silence, all looked to the leader. Spaggiari smiled—and then announced dinner. The tired gang members looked at one another, silently questioning the sanity of their leader. The Frenchman magically produced liver pâté, fruit, salami, cheeses, soup, and ripe grapes; he had even brought a gas burner for warming the food. Laughter erupted all around as the men enjoyed the dinner break to revive their strength and maintain their spirits. This meal would capture headlines

The venerable Société Generale Bank boasted a vault so fortified that its insurer, Lloyd's of London, did not require the French bank to add electronic sensor alarms. The bank and Lloyd's did not figure on a bold subterranean assault.

around the world and put a particularly
French touch to this masterful caper.

Refreshed and again under control, the
men started upon twenty-four hours of
looting safes and safe-deposit boxes. The
work stopped only once when a thief
heard noises and called to the others to be
still. Spaggiari breezed toward the area
where the noise was heard: the night depository. A bag of cash glided down the
chute from street level right into the
leader's arms: a cool $175,000 from a local
casino. The men went back to work.

A jeweler joined the gang in the wee
hours of Monday morning to assess the
value of the jewelry piling up in the middle of the floor. He bagged the best of the
stuff and left through the tunnel. With
dawn rapidly approaching, Spaggiari assigned some of the men to start loading
the gold onto the rafts to be floated back
to the Land-Rover. The sewer train became busy again as time began to run
short. At 5:00 A.M. Spaggiari ordered the
looting to cease. They had opened only
four hundred of the four thousand safe-
deposit boxes, but the entire take was already worth more than six million dollars.
The thieves left their tools and nearly two
million dollars in negotiable bonds and re-
jected valuables littering the floor. All
lookouts, tunnelers, and loot were out of
the sewers safely before the sun rose.

A few hours later, when the great vault
door failed to open, no one suspected a
robbery. By midafternoon, locksmiths had

abandoned trying to open the door. When they punched a hole through the wall by the door, they saw that the problem was not a mechanical difficulty and promptly discovered that the Société Generale bank had been robbed.

In addition to the painted slogan *"Sans armes, sans haine, et sans violence,"* the police found several pornographic photos of local big shots taped to the walls—no doubt taken from a not-so-safe-deposit box. They also found an elegantly engraved silver bowl filled with human excrement; the ways of thieves are often filthy, but this detail was beyond the usual. A plethora of evidence was left behind, but not a single fingerprint or clue could lead to the perpetrators of the crime. The police were stumped.

Aftermath

A few months after the robbery, in an act of desperation, the police cast a broad dragnet and rounded up scores of local crooks in hopes of scaring up some information about the crime. They unknowingly nabbed a couple of the lower-ranked members of the gang, who confessed in a sudden fit of panic. These thieves pointed fingers at Spaggiari, and he was immediately arrested.

After thirty-six straight hours of interrogation, Spaggiari would not admit to anything and remained the picture of calm. Not until police threatened to arrest his wife did Spaggiari consent to cooperate. Very little of the loot had turned up and few other gang members had been apprehended. Spaggiari was the state's only real hope.

For weeks, sessions with a local judge and lawyer meant to gather information about the robbery dragged on, with Spaggiari being evasive and filling the pages of the court reporter's transcripts with obvious lies. All the meetings took place in the same small second-story room in the hall of justice, and the participants grew quite familiar with one another. On the day of the twentieth session, Spaggiari arose from his chair and went to the window. When he stepped outside, all feared he was going to commit suicide by throwing himself to the pavement below. They leapt from their chairs and gasped as Spaggiari jumped from the ledge. The judge and others rushed to the window to see Spaggiari land on the roof of a car, leap to the rear of a motorcycle, and be whisked away by the waiting driver. It is the last any official has ever seen of the man. His wife has vanished as well.

Spaggiari has been heard from only twice: once to pay the owner of the car on which he landed during his escape for the damage he caused, and once, a few years later, to send a postcard to some French reporters to confirm that he was indeed alive. The take from the robbery was between six and eighteen million dollars—banks do not usually divulge exact amounts, and deposit-box owners are often secretive about what they hide away—and less than $250,000 has ever been recovered. It is believed that Albert Spaggiari deposited his share of the loot in Japan. Most of the gang is still at large.

The Nice job remains the largest and most successful single bank robbery in history. But it would be wrong to think banks are the only things on the minds of the world's most daring thieves. There are plenty of places where wealth accumulates besides banks, and none is completely safe.

chapter

TWO

PLANES, TRAINS, AND AUTO- MOBILES

Money and valuables, of course, do not remain forever hidden within the vaults of the world's banks. Gold and currency must move between nations, corporations, and private citizens, and when it does, it is vulnerable. Even though train cars have been equipped with safes and guards, automobiles have been armored, and planes seem naturally impregnable, thieves have found their way to penetrate these modes of transportation and dip their hands into the riches of others.

Trains

Although the very first train robbery was an inside job pulled off in England in the mid-1800s, holding up trains was practically an American pastime for the next seventy years. Historians point out that America's great open spaces provided plentiful opportunity for thieves to hold up trains as they crossed the country.

Moreover, some historical psychologists believe the crime was so popular in the United States because many robbers were simply trying to break up the crushing boredom of life on the prairies, which offered little beyond farm chores and watching cows. Even if that theory is true, the professional outlaw was still a very significant factor in railroad crime; in fact, the whole American experience was begun by seasoned outlaws.

As easy as banks were to hit, trains proved to be an even easier ticket to elicit profit after the Civil War. Specifically, it was the express cars that traveled a few

Trendsetter John Reno (right) was one of the members of the Reno Gang that took a break from terrorizing the citizens of Seymour, Indiana, to pull off America's first train robbery in 1866. Twenty-eight years later, scenes like the one pictured in the above engraving were happening more than twice a week in the American West. No one could stop the epidemic of train robberies.

cars behind the locomotive that brightened the eyes of the train robber. These cars were privately owned by companies like Adams and American Express and contained valuable cargo, payroll shipments, and cash transfers, which the express companies carried for a fee.

On October 6, 1866, the Reno Gang stopped a train outside of Seymour, Indiana, and robbed the express car, stealing the contents of one safe and carrying another safe off into the night to be cracked open at their leisure. Four days later, a train near Bristow, Kentucky, was intentionally derailed so robbers could make off with $8,000. When the Reno Gang

struck again in Indiana, they scored between $40,000 and $170,000 (between the gang's bragging and the express company's prevarications, it has been difficult for historians to pin down the exact amount that was taken).

It was not long before trains all over the West were being stopped, derailed, or completely destroyed in a rash of virtually unstoppable robberies. Jesse and Frank James derailed their first train near Adair, Iowa, on July 21, 1873, causing engineer John Rafferty to be scalded to death and his fireman to be badly burned. The James brothers got away with $26,000, and people riding trains began doing so in fear.

The Tehachapi train wreck brought about the deaths of fifteen helpless passengers— the tragic result of an attempted railway robbery.

Train Wreckers

In January 1883, on a train ascending Tehachapi Summit in the California Sierras, robbers separated the rear seven cars from the locomotive, hoping to hold up the passengers. But when the brakes failed to work, the cars careened backward down the steep incline to become a nightmarish roller coaster. Traveling at a speed faster than seventy miles per hour (112kph), the train derailed and then disintegrated into a roiling mass of twisted steel and splintered wood, obliterating the fifteen passengers who were trapped inside.

The Resurrection Ruse

Twice in history, train robbers have had themselves shipped in coffins in express cars with the hopes of emerging Draculalike from their pine boxes to rob the train. On the Union Pacific out of Ogden, Utah, in 1879, the express-car messenger heard a rustling in a coffin and shot the robber dead as he opened the casket. Seventeen years later in Wisconsin, another express-car messenger became suspicious of the coffin he was riding along with, so he placed a bunch of heavy packages on top of it. At the next stop, he and the local sheriff loudly threatened to empty their revolvers into the coffin; this broke the courage of the thief within who cried, "I'm in here, don't shoot!"

Train wrecks caused by robbers became so common in the nineteenth century that passengers began vying for seats in the middle cars in the belief that those cars would be the safest place on the train in the event of a derailment. Railroad companies beefed up security and express companies armed their clerks, but train robbery remained epidemic. Unlike the romantic highwaymen of old Europe, these train robbers were widely despised by the general public because of the horrific wrecks they caused.

The very worst of the robber wrecks occurred in Alabama two days after Christmas in 1896. A derailment killed twenty-seven of the thirty-five travelers aboard, who had set out to enjoy a holiday excursion. When the robbers realized they had derailed a train with no express or freight cars to rob, they contented themselves with rummaging through the baggage and pockets of the dead and dying passengers.

Like bank robbery, train robbery survived into the new century despite the success of lawmen at tracking down thieves. One lawman named Alan Pinkerton pioneered modern police methods by the practices of keeping accurate notes on file, observing criminal patterns, and spending money on informants. Pinkerton knew there was little honor among thieves, and many bank and train robbers were apprehended based on tips that he had secured from their criminal brethren. Even so, trains continued to be robbed all the way through the Roaring Twenties, leading up to the biggest American train robbery in history.

America's Biggest: Simple and Inside

On June 13, 1924, at Roundout, Illinois, bandits stepped out from their hiding spots in the engine cab of a moving locomotive. The engineer was ordered to stop the train at a preplanned spot, where more bandits emerged from the trees to fire gas-releasing canisters into the mail car. Postal workers opened the doors to get out, and the thieves, wearing gas masks, rushed in to grab sixty-three registered mail sacks and run back out into the night. In just a few moments, the robbers had made off with two million dollars in cash, leaving not a single clue. Police and federal inspectors were stumped until a phone call tipped them off that a leading postal inspector had been in on the heist. Within a month the gang was in jail and most of the money recovered.

America's Last: Simpletons with Guns

By 1937, train robbery was a mellowing memory in the American consciousness, the stuff of daydreams and movies. Henry Lorenz and his friend Harry Dwyer were foolish enough to believe the dreams and the movies, however, and they set off from Chicago during that Depression year in search of an Old West that was long gone. The young men caught a train to El Paso, Texas, where they headed straight for a clothing store to purchase new outfits for the adventure ahead. They sauntered out of the store decked out in duds they had seen in the movies but the likes of which probably had never been seen in the real West: big Stetsons, bandannas, boots, and shining belt buckles the size of Cadillac hubcaps.

The greenhorns, no doubt, drew laughs from the locals; the two dreamers never noticed that El Paso was much more like the cities they had left behind in the East than the Dodge City and Tombstone landscapes they had seen in the movies. After a short, unhappy attempt at living off the land on horseback, Harry and Henry decided to undertake a different kind of Old West endeavor; they decided that they would rob the Southern Pacific's westbound Apache Limited.

The two men, still attracting snickers in their cowboy garb, boarded the train in El Paso shortly after midnight. After waiting until they were well away from the city and they were sure that most of the passengers were asleep in their seats, Henry drew a pistol in the aisle of the passenger car and announced their intentions. Supported by the authority of Henry's shaking gun, Harry started collecting money and jewelry from the sleepy and surprised passengers. One man resisted, and Henry shot him in the leg; whatever comedy there had been in this scene faded rapidly. Just as it looked like the two

Harry Dwyer (second from left) and Henry Lorenz (third from left) in police custody after being beaten into subjugation by the passengers aboard the train they attempted to rob.

novices were going to succeed at the caper, another passenger, W.L. Smith, grabbed Henry and wrestled him to the floor of the aisle. Other men on the coach jumped to Smith's aid. In the ensuing skirmish, the gun went off again, seriously wounding Smith, but by now the passengers had gained the upper hand, and only the intervention of the women passengers prevented the men from killing Harry and Henry with their fists.

Western train robbery ended forever with this funny yet sad story that took place on a train in the middle of nowhere. The English, however, inventors of the train robbery, were to be heard from one more spectacular time.

The Great Train Robbery

What the British had begun nearly a century before, they ended on August 8, 1963. It had been decades since anyone had robbed a train—even in the wild and woolly American West—so when the express train from Glasgow to London

slowed to a stop in the English hinterland not far from a place called Cheddington in Buckinghamshire, no one aboard suspected it was the beginning of a robbery.

The engineer had brought the train to a stop because the light signals beside the tracks showed red. When the engineer left the locomotive to take a look down the track, he did not get far; he and his assistant were beset by masked bandits wielding pick handles padded with cloth (this was, after all, a British operation; only Americans resorted to guns). The bandits, who had rigged the red lights that had brought the train to a stop, now separated the engine and the first few cars from the rest of the train and started to drive them slowly away into the night.

Among the front cars was a postal coach filled with clerks who sorted the mail as the train made its passage southward. Stops and starts were not rare events on this long haul and the clerks within the mail car suspected nothing. The robbers stopped the train a second time at a small bridge over a road before breaking into the lightly secured mail car. Faced by determined men armed with clubs, the clerks yielded control of the car to the bandits after only brief resistance.

With the situation firmly in hand, the thieves turned their attention to a row of lockers overflowing with white canvas bags. Each bag was stuffed with British currency being sent from Scottish banks to England to be exchanged for Scottish currency. In minutes, 128 bags weighing more than two tons (1.8t) and containing £2,131,000 were whisked hand to hand along a chain of bandits from the train car into a caravan composed of a military truck and Land-Rovers that was waiting in the road beneath the bridge.

The Great Train Robbery. Precious few clues were left behind by the crew of thieves who shocked Britain with their audacious raid on a train. In fact, not a single usable clue was left at the scene of the crime.

As the military-looking convoy (the thieves had changed into army uniforms) pulled away down the narrow country road and into the darkness, the clerks were left stranded in the middle of nowhere, miles from even a telephone. In the hours that it took another train to come upon the scene and the word to get to London that there had been a huge crime, the robbers could have driven miles away. Instead, they chose to hide out in a nearby farm compound, called Leatherslade Farm, which they had secured in advance to use as a staging area and hideout. The farmhouse was stockpiled with food, reading material, a few games, and cotton gloves (to prevent their leaving fingerprints) in anticipation of the gang holing up there for the days immediately following the heist. The plan was to wait out the initial response to the robbery and then disperse when the search widened beyond the area.

The thieves were largely a London crew, led by Bruce Richard Reynolds, composed of professionals having long associations with various London crime families. For the first few days after the robbery, the gang acted according to plan by staying in the hideout and playing cards, reading cheap novels, and playing Monopoly with real money. They knew that the police were aware that they had had hours to escape, and they expected the focus of the police would soon shift to the big cities far away. Although they had reasonable expectations of police procedure, Scotland Yard decided to do the exact opposite. The police were convinced, albeit by very little evidence, that the train robbers were still in the area and began a house-to-house search. When the thieves realized they were in the middle of a closing net, they broke from their original plan and decided to vacate the farm days ahead of schedule.

Police were tipped off about strange goings-on at Leatherslade Farm by a neighboring farmer but ignored the lead! Still, they happened upon the scene in time to find the few valuable clues that would later lead to convictions of the gang.

Coat and tie required. The Big Four of the Great Train Robbery were Bruce Reynolds (1), capo of London's Southwest Gang crime organization; Charles Wilson (8), greengrocer, small-time bookie and leading schemer; Ronald "Buster" Edwards (3), capo of London's Southeast Gang; and Douglas Gordon Goody (4), hairdresser with a violent streak and a head for planning ahead. The four planned the robbery, recruited the gang from a pool of professionals, and assembled the necessary resources. Also pictured are safe and lock man James White (2), arrested when a policeman found £30,000 behind a loose panel on his house trailer; Thomas Wisby (7), convicted by a single fingerprint found at Leatherslade Farm; William Boal (6), captured when he extravagantly spent some of the fresh loot; and James Hussey (5), a painter convicted because of a palm print left on the getaway truck.

By leaving the farm early, the gang sacrificed the day set aside to thoroughly clean up the premises. Reynolds, the ringleader, hired a man outside the gang to travel to the farmhouse and do the cleanup job after the train robbers had left. By the time Reynolds got the horrifying news that the man had never shown up at Leatherslade Farm, however, it was too late to hire another. The police inspected the farmhouse and found plenty of evidence that it had been the gang's hideout—white canvas bags and some of the equipment

TOP: *Charles Wilson being led to trial in chains. He managed to escape prison by paying two men to break in and get him out. He was tracked down in Canada and reincarcerated in 1968.*

BOTTOM: *Bruce Reynolds went the longest without being arrested by living abroad until his arrest in England in 1968. When the police burst in upon him, Reynolds merely shrugged and remarked, "C'est la vie."*

used to rob the train were carelessly strewn around the place. They combed the place for fingerprints and found enough scattered around the house to identify most of the gang.

All the robbers, as far as is known, were apprehended, although less than an eighth of the loot was ever recovered. Two members of the gang, Reynolds and Ronald Biggs, successfully eluded the police for years. Reynolds, who was identi-

Road to Rio. Pictured here in 1985, Ronald Biggs escaped from prison in England in 1965. The only at-large member of the Great Train Robbery Gang, Biggs has made a life for himself in Brazil. His celebrity has led to jobs appearing naked in a magazine foldout, making ads for running shoes, and taking to the air waves in 1992 to advise visitors to the Earth Summit in Rio de Janeiro on the hazards of local crime.

fied by a single fingerprint found on the Monopoly board (another member left a single print on a dish he used to feed a stray cat), was finally arrested in 1968.

Biggs was arrested earlier than Reynolds but managed to escape the authorities and abscond to Brazil. Once in South America, Biggs fathered a child with a Brazilian woman and used an obscure nineteenth-century law that protects parents of natives from deportation and extradition. The controversy made the untouchable Biggs a headline hero in his old homeland, as the last outlaw still free after the last and biggest train robbery the world has ever seen.

From Train Cars to Armored Cars

Although train robbery slacked off in America, overland robbery in other forms did not endure the same fate. The armored-car security industry started in 1923 when an enterprising Chicago man fortified a school bus with steel plates and began leasing it out to those who needed to transport large sums of money. His idea was the beginning of something huge. The amount of money being trucked about on the streets is truly astounding; any one of the prominent New York City armored-car services hauls an average of $500 million *a day*. At the other end of the spectrum, carriers who limit their hauls to $250,000 a run in order to deter theft are considered merely penny-ante outfits. The United States experiences about three armored-car heists every two weeks, and the phenomenon is by no means strictly limited to America.

Britain's Way

Like the rest of the world, London is not immune to armored-car robbery. On May 1, 1967, a highly organized group of thieves ambushed a Commers van carrying gold bars to customers around the city. On Bowling Green Lane, one of the three guards, Jack Chandler, left the van to make a routine drop but was jumped and overwhelmed on his way back to the van. When the guards in the rear of the vehicle

TOP: *Heavy metal thunder. The armor, independent ventilating systems that guard against gas assault, electric doors that limit access, and high-tech radio and telephone communications are not adequate to stop the bane of the armored-car industry—the inside job.*

BOTTOM: *From left to right, Richard Brew, Walter Clements, and John Chandler, the three security guards bound and blindfolded during the Bowling Green Lane robbery.*

heard a knock on the door, they opened the rear entrance expecting Chandler but received a blast of ammonia-smelling spray in the eyes instead. Rendered blind, choking, and helpless, the three guards were easily bound and blindfolded.

With the guards in the back of the van, one of the thieves navigated the vehicle through noonday traffic to a designated spot, where the gang transferred 140 three-pound (1.3kg) gold bars into waiting vehicles. After the thieves had gone, the guards kicked the walls of the van and shouted until they were rescued by passing women. The operation from start to finish took less than an hour and netted the robbers $2.5 million in gold. The case remains unsolved.

The Bowling Green Lane robbery is a prime example of how most armored-car jobs are carried out. The thieves in that robbery had spent days observing the habits of one particular truck they suspected would carry the most attractive payload. They knew that the best time to hit the vehicle was when it had stopped for a delivery and the guards were split between duties. Lastly, the thieves knew the tedious routine of the guards might make them just careless enough to give the thieves an opening: the knock they used on the van door sounded like Chandler's usual knock, so the guards opened the door unprepared.

To counter these threats, armored-courier companies—at least the conscientious ones—take many precautions in addition to bulletproof walls and windows, mine-resistant flooring, and gas-proof ventilation to deter thieves. Many trucks maintain constant radio contact while on the road for immediate reporting of attempted robberies. Some companies alter their pickup schedules and personnel to keep them fresh and less predictable. Sometimes these tactics work, and sometimes they do not.

Two Vegas Jackpots

Two robberies pulled off in Las Vegas—probably by the same bandits—against the Loomis armored-car service make excellent examples of how the average armored-car heist comes off in the United States. On October 1, 1993, a gunman in the ubiquitous ski mask crept up on the driver of a Loomis truck parked in front of the MGM Grand Hotel for a pickup. The driver was ordered to move the truck to another location, where the money was transferred to a second vehicle. The take was $2.9 million.

Three months later, another Loomis truck that had stopped at the Circus Circus Resort vanished with its driver while her colleagues were inside the resort filling automated teller machines. The van was later recovered, but the driver and $3.1 million are still missing. Police believe the two Vegas jobs are related and suspect that the missing driver was an accomplice in the theft rather than a victim. The take in each of these jobs was about average for what armored-car robberies yield. The possibility that the heist was an inside job makes it similar to perhaps 70 percent of the other armored-car rip-offs in America.

The Biggest Armored-Car Theft

The largest holdup ever of an armored car took place in a suburb of New York City in June 1991. An Armored Motor Services truck pulled up to a convenience store so that one of the two guards could buy sandwiches and coffee. When the guard returned to the truck, she found the driver being held at gunpoint and herself helpless. The driver was forced to drive to another location, where $10.8 million was loaded into another vehicle.

The FBI has reportedly long suspected the driver of the van, Albert M. Ranieri, of being involved in the job. In fact, the FBI suspects Ranieri's father, Albert B. Ranieri, of being in on the crime as well, but the Bureau has been unable to prove its case despite thousands of hours of surveillance and investigation. Even if the Ranieris did commit the crime, the statute of limitations for armored-car robbery runs out at the end of five years; however, IRS laws about not reporting income have no statute of limitations.

Air Pirates

Planes offer a unique problem for the modern highwayman—the means of escape. Trains and other overland methods of transportation allow the robber to pick his spot for the holdup with an eye to an effective way to get away. Leaving a plane in flight is not an endeavor to be undertaken lightly, however, and for this reason, robbers usually victimize airplane passengers using extortionist methods.

The masked figure holding a gun to the head of a pilot or flight attendant evokes universal loathing in many people's minds; terrorism is an international scourge surpassing the evil of mere criminality. The only successful terrorist extortion in history took place in October 1977 when a JAL DC-8 was taken in Bangladesh with thirty-eight hostages aboard. Japan paid six million dollars in ransom and set six convicted criminals free to meet the demands of the gunmen aboard the plane. The Bangladesh government, which also acceded to the terrorists' demands, has refused to sanction action against the extortionists, who remain at large and unpunished.

The One That Got Away—Maybe

In the United States, one airplane hijacker has eluded the acrimony usually afforded men and women who commandeer planes at gunpoint for the purpose of extortion: D.B. Cooper. Cooper—the name an alias—boarded Northwest flight 305 in

Northwest flight 305. D.B. Cooper allowed the plane to land only after assurances that the money and parachutes he had demanded were ready to go. Cooper evidently wanted to minimize the opportunity for authorities to assault the airliner while it was on the ground.

Portland, Oregon, on November 24, 1971, and took a seat in the last row of the plane. Once the plane was in the air and heading to Seattle, Cooper began chain-smoking Raleigh cigarettes. He summoned flight attendant Florence Schaffner to his seat, showed her what appeared to be a bomb, and then gave the surprised attendant a note typed on the front of a five-by-seven-inch (12.7 by 17.7cm) envelope: MISS—I HAVE A BOMB HERE, AND I WOULD LIKE YOU TO SIT BY ME. How could she refuse?

Using Schaffner to carry pretyped messages forward to the cockpit, Cooper demanded that $200,000 and two parachutes be delivered to the plane once it landed in Seattle. When the police delivered the parachutes and money, Cooper surprised the officials by releasing all thirty-five passengers and two of the stewardesses, to whom he offered generous tips (they refused). Cooper ordered the plane into the sky with directions to fly over the vast, unpopulated western United States toward Mexico City far to the south.

Cooper had chosen his plane carefully; the Northwest Orient jet was a Boeing 727-100 with a rear-lowering staircase located beneath the tail, which could be operated from the passenger compartment. With the crew locked away in the cockpit up front, Cooper checked the parachutes before attaching them and the money to his body and opening the rear door of the plane. Somewhere, probably over southwestern Washington, Cooper leapt into the night and was never heard from again. Although a light in the cockpit signaled to the pilot that the door had been opened, there was no way

Cool-headed flight attendant Florence Schaffner ferried notes to and from the cockpit for Cooper. She refused a two-thousand-dollar tip that Cooper offered her when she was allowed to leave the plane with passengers.

to tell exactly where along the flight path Cooper had jumped.

The only material clues Cooper left behind were a clip-on tie and a mother-of-pearl tiepin, both found on the seat where Cooper probably changed into his jumpsuit. Of the ten thousand twenty-dollar bills Cooper received as ransom and whose serial numbers were meticulously recorded by FBI agents, only $5,880 has ever turned up. These bills were found buried, inexplicably, near the Columbia River in Washington State. The rest seem to have never been spent, which has led authorities to suspect that Cooper may not have lived long after the heist.

In the early reporting of the hijacking, Cooper's name was incorrectly listed as "D.B.," even though the passenger list showed him as "Dan" Cooper. Perhaps preferring the mystery of the initials, the legend makers have never abandoned "D.B." for the simple and straightforward "Dan." The skydiver's guts and cleverness—and the fact that he left all aboard unharmed—have allowed Cooper to sidestep the particularly keen hatred that the public usually reserves for hijackers. Only a brave few have ever attempted to reproduce his crime.

Cooper Redux?

In April 1972, another man tried Cooper's game under the alias of James Johnson, only to be revealed as a former Green Beret and distinguished soldier named Richard McCoy. Brandishing a pistol and a hand grenade, McCoy hijacked a United Airlines flight traveling from Denver to Los Angeles. Johnson's brief note to the stewardess, interestingly, was typed on a

five-by-seven-inch (12.7 by 17.7cm) envelope and read as follows: GRENADE PIN PULLED, PISTOL LOADED. Inside the envelope were detailed instructions, starting with the demand that the plane be diverted to San Francisco.

Once on the ground, McCoy demanded half a million dollars and four parachutes, even though he had brought his own chute in a carry-on bag; McCoy planned to use the chutes provided by the police and almost surely wired with transmitters as decoys. McCoy ordered the Boeing 727 into the night sky and directed the pilot through written instructions to

Have to turn it in, son. Brian Ingram, age eight, shows where he discovered the only portion of Cooper's loot ever to turn up. The decrepit condition of the bills led authorities to believe they had remained buried since the heist, but Cooper enthusiasts like to claim that the money was planted to deceive investigators.

TOP: *The ears have it. In addition to a similar clip-on tie and tiepin, Richard McCoy shared a physical trait with D.B. Cooper: Cooper's ears were described as enormous, and McCoy's nickname around Salt Lake City was "Dumbo."*

BOTTOM: *Feds combed the bank of the Columbia River where a little boy discovered some of the Cooper haul, but found no trace of the rest of the $200,000 ransom.*

fly a zigzag path over the western United States. When McCoy found that his own parachute was unusable, he had no choice but to use one of the government parachutes, which was indeed wired to give away his location. He jumped into the night near Provo, Utah, and miraculously eluded capture. Police were just as stymied in this caper as they were in the Cooper case—until they got a break.

McCoy made the error of speculating about what it would take to pull off such a job in idle conversation with his classmates at Brigham Young University in Salt Lake City. Since the class they were sharing was a course in law enforcement, McCoy probably should have guessed that the lawmen taking the course might later suspect him of such a crime. One of

the policemen with whom McCoy had chattered later went to FBI agents, who were able to take a fingerprint that matched McCoy's off an in-flight magazine and arrest the hijacker. McCoy was convicted and sentenced to forty-five years in federal prison.

McCoy's incredible story does not end there, however, because he escaped from prison, only to be eventually trapped and gunned down by federal agents when he resisted recapture. One of the agents involved in the case believes that McCoy and D. B. Cooper are the same man since they look somewhat alike and used similar methods. And there is further evidence pointing to this conclusion. McCoy's family members confirmed that he had a clipon tie and tiepin like the one Cooper left behind, and McCoy's whereabouts during the Cooper heist are very suspicious. Still, the case against McCoy is not easily proved. Would the careful planner of the first heist have bumbled so badly in the second one? Might McCoy merely be a copycat hijacker? No matter what the truth, McCoy never confessed to the Cooper job, and if he indeed is the one who pulled it off, he was stoic enough to take the secret to his grave.

The police sketches of Cooper, who used heavy make-up to darken his complexion and donned mirrored sunglasses to hide his eyes. The Cooper case is still open.

TOP: *Anthony Pino, self-pro-fessed head of the Brinks Gang, was arrested just a few days before the statute of limitations would have made him safe from the law.*

BOTTOM: *When men wore hats and streets were dark at night. Investigators marvel that the fortresslike Brinks warehouse could have been robbed of so much so fast— more than a million in cash in about seventeen minutes.*

Warehouse Jobs

Money and valuables in transit are not just vulnerable in trucks, trains, and airplanes. Some of the world's biggest capers have happened in warehouses where loot piles up waiting for its next move.

Brinks

The grandfather of all brilliantly planned and meticulously executed heists was the famed Brinks warehouse robbery, carried out January 17, 1950, in Boston, Massachusetts. Tony Pino and his gang had been terrorizing Brinks trucks for months when they decided to go for the big tomato—the warehouse itself. In the weeks leading up to the heist, Pino's gang broke into the warehouse offices seventy-five times to reconnoiter and make keys for all the door locks; went to Washington, D.C., to study the patent drawings of the vault and alarm systems; calculated which day of the week would be best for the hit by timing how long the lights were on in the counting room each night (the longer they were on, the more money was being counted in the warehouse); and had a special truck made up that could be loaded inconspicuously from the side to minimize the amount of time the thieves would have to spend in the open when they made their getaway.

On the appointed winter night, eleven thieves wearing Halloween masks, chauffeur caps, and navy jackets struck the warehouse. They moved easily through doors and down corridors, opening every lock with the appropriate key. At the counting room, the bandits ordered the startled guards and accountants to the floor, where the thieves quickly bound them. The robbers then stuffed canvas bags with $1,218,211.29 in cash and

Tough guys. Members of the Brinks Gang, all professionals with underworld connections, gave lessons on how to clam up in the hands of the cops. All were convicted and did not see freedom again until they were old men.

Nothing for the Brinks man to pick up. Jimmy Burke's gang had already made off with $5 million in cash and almost $1 million in jewels. By leaving a trail of corpses rather than witnesses, Burke eluded arrest for the Lufthansa heist.

$1,557,187.83 in checks before rushing to their getaway truck outside. The whole operation took a mere seventeen minutes and came off without a single hitch.

A manhunt that cost the United States government $29 million yielded nothing for police agencies. Years passed without an arrest in the case. As the statute of limitations approached in 1956, one Joseph "Specs" O'Keefe went to the police and ratted the whole gang out. O'Keefe, one member of the gang that pulled the heist, had been denied his share of the loot and made good his threat to turn stool pigeon if the rest of the gang would not give him his due. All eight remaining thieves (some had already died) were convicted and sentenced to life imprisonment; none was freed until all were very old men.

The Lufthansa Job

Jimmy Burke, who ran the theft industry around Kennedy Airport in New York City for two decades, was a tough charac-

ter who had literally grown up on the streets of Brooklyn when he was not being shuffled from one foster home to another. As a man, he directed two of the biggest warehouse burglaries in history (if you have seen the movie *Goodfellas*, Burke is the character portrayed by Robert De Niro). In 1967, after paying a prostitute to seduce the head of security so that they could steal and duplicate the only key to the security area of Air France's warehouse, Burke's gang pillaged the vaults of the warehouse and made off with more than $1 million in cash.

Eleven years later, Burke and company struck again at Kennedy and set a record for cash theft. With his connections to the reigning Mafia family in the area, Burke operated with enormous amounts of inside information passed on to him from airport employees who were either looking to score themselves or to get out from under gambling debts owed to the Mafia. Through the mob grapevine, Burke generally knew what was being shipped to and from the airport by both land and air.

Louis Werner, a cargo supervisor for Lufthansa, passed word to the mob that huge amounts of cash were flown periodically into the airport from Europe, and that the money was kept overnight at the Lufthansa warehouse until the banks opened the next day. Werner passed detailed information about the security setup and general layout of the Lufthansa warehouse to a mobster known as Joe "Buddha" Manri (nicknamed for his girth rather than religious faith), who then passed the tip on to Burke and his gang.

On December 11, 1978, nearly a dozen gunmen descended on the warehouse at 3:12 A.M. They systematically took control of the entire operation. First, they smacked an outside security guard on the head with a pistol and ordered him to turn off the silent alarm system at the warehouse gate. Timing their attack to catch practically the entire staff at their meal break in the lunchroom, the gunmen entered the room and ordered the Lufthansa workers to stop chewing and get on the floor. They then led senior manager Rudi Eirich through the maze of passages to the vault, where they ordered him to unlock the door. (The thieves knew exactly where the vault was and even how its tricky double alarm worked: there were two doors one had to pass through to get to the valuable cargo. If someone opened the second door without closing the first door, a silent alarm would alert authorities.) Eirich was told to keep his hand away from a hidden alarm switch in the vault safe. Thorough planning and precise information allowed the gang to get straight to the heart of the Lufthansa warehouse without hitting a single snag. The robbers carried off forty parcels con-

Another Brinks fortress stormed. The Brinks Mat warehouse near Heathrow was thought to be impervious to thieves—no more than the Titanic was to icebergs.

taining $5 million in untraceable cash and $875,000 in jewels.

Because of the precise information possessed by the gang, the police suspected the robbery to be an inside job and were not long in arresting Louis Werner and pressuring him to name names. Knowing Joe "Buddha" Manri was the only member of the gang Werner had had direct contact with, Burke was swift and merciless in cutting off any connection between himself and potential stool pigeon Werner; Manri was murdered, making it nearly impossible for the police to build a case against Burke. According to a government informant, Burke further insulated himself from prosecution by killing other gang members in addition to Manri. Although authorities have little doubt about Burke's guilt, the case is officially classified as unsolved and the money has never been recovered. Burke is in prison serving time for other charges and will probably remain there for the rest of his life.

The Brinks Job—British Style

The scale of Burke's Lufthansa job was dwarfed five years later in 1983, when a large band of English thieves hit London's Heathrow Airport for a haul worth more than $50 million. Six armed men entered the airport facility of Brinks Mat Ltd. on November 26 at 6:40 A.M., the precise moment the guard shift was changing and the alarms were necessarily turned off. Once the thieves were inside the offices and in control of the staff, they needed the employees' cooperation in order to open the vault, which they got by dousing one of the guards with gasoline and threatening to burn him to death if the vault was not

opened immediately. The tactic worked, and the thieves gained access to a vast treasure in gold.

With the guards bound and blindfolded, others joined the assault group to load out the three tons (2.7t) of gold the gang stole in the form of 6,800 bars. In less than an hour the thieves moved the immense weight in bullion—and more than $200,000 in diamonds—out of the vault and made their getaway. The take was so big that international gold prices were adversely affected.

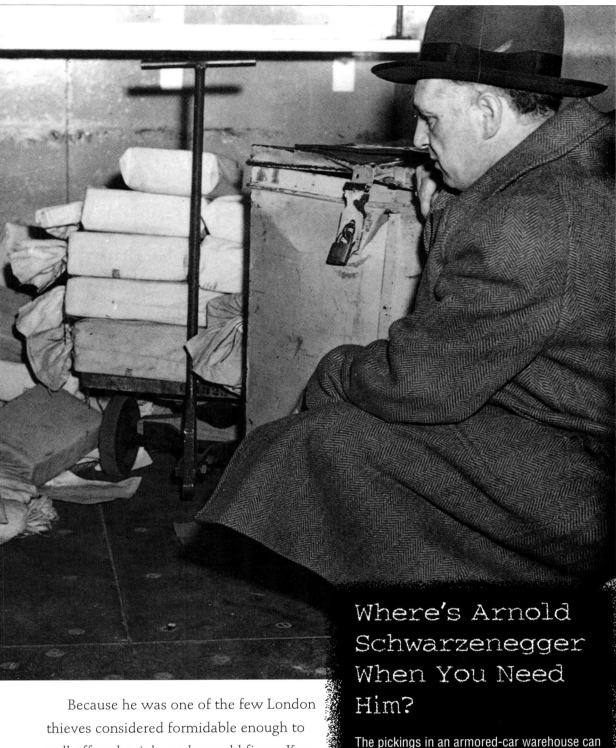

Keep the change. A Boston detective surveys what the Brinks Gang left behind in 1950—mostly coins, still generally considered too cumbersome to carry off.

Because he was one of the few London thieves considered formidable enough to pull off such a job, underworld figure Kenneth Noye became Scotland Yard's prime suspect. The Yard's suspicions that Noye was the mastermind proved well founded, for he was arrested after killing an inspector working the case. Along with five others, Noye was convicted for his part in the robbery. However, the police can only claim partial success in this case since at least ten thieves remain at large and more than half the loot is still unrecovered.

Where's Arnold Schwarzenegger When You Need Him?

The pickings in an armored-car warehouse can be so rich that frequently more is left behind than is taken. The Brooklyn warehouse of the Hudson Armored Car Company was robbed by three thieves in 1992. After getting the drop on the night guard, the men stole $8 million in hundred-dollar bills but left $30 million behind. Since the loot they actually carried off only weighed 120 pounds (54.4kg), investigators concluded the thieves were either weak or stupid, or just plain got scared and took off. The crime remains unsolved. The police suspect that the robbery was an inside job.

BOSTON POLICE

GARD

A DA VINCI TO CALL ONE'S OWN

Art is the medium of expression that pre-dates writing by centuries. Some see art as the very soul of a civilization, its most articulate and enduring voice that gives illumination and shading to the spectrum of human experience from love and hate to reason and madness. Others, less high-minded perhaps, want to rip it off, forge it, or use it only as a medium of transferring dollars, deutsche marks, and yen from the unwary to their own pockets. Vases, paintings, and sculpture are much more than merely means of expression—they are coveted merchandise, the objects of insatiable greed and passion, and prey for thieves and con artists.

Artful Dodges: Forgers

When the sculptor Michelangelo was a young man, he participated in an art scam at the behest of his powerful patron, Lorenzo de' Medici. Medici ordered the young artist to carve a sleeping cupid, which he then had buried in acidic soil to stain and pit the stone. Then, through an art dealer, Medici sold the sculpture to Catholic Cardinal Riario of San Giorgio, who thought he was buying a piece of fifteen-hundred-year-old Greek history. Michelangelo's cut was 15 percent of the sale price of two hundred gold ducats.

Rumors about the deception eventually reached the cardinal, who angrily demanded his money back. Lorenzo de' Medici denied any part in the scheme, but Michelangelo happily confessed, proud his work had been mistaken for that of one of the Greek masters of antiquity. The cardinal was refunded his gold, and he lives in history as a man too clever to be duped into buying an original Michelangelo.

Some modern artists have turned their hands to forgery in an attempt to get back at an art world that has wounded them. Playing down or perhaps rationalizing the lucrative payoffs they received for their forgeries, artists who have chosen the shadier road claim to have used forgery to finally prove their own talents or expose the dirtier side of the legitimate art world. Or at least that is what they tell the police.

Dutch Threat

One of the spurned artists who resorted to forgery was Hans van Meegeren, who deeply resented the art critics of Europe for ignoring his work and belittling his talents. The eccentric Dutchman turned his back on the art world and moved to the French Riviera to live in seclusion. His life in seclusion became a good deal more comfortable, however, when he "discovered" a lost Vermeer painting, *Supper at Emmaus*, in 1937. The painting was enthusiastically authenticated as a lost treasure by an aging expert of impeccable integrity, and van Meegeren sold it for the present-day equivalent of two million dollars.

Over the next few years more Vermeers popped up, much to the delight of the art world and the material gratification of van Meegeren. Even World War II did not stop art activity on the continent. Nazi Hermann Göring actually took a break from directing the blitz against London and looting the museums of Europe to buy a painting from van Meegeren. The notable war criminal purchased a long lost Vermeer, *Christ and the Adulteress*, which had found its way into the Dutch artist's hands. But the sale, however lucrative, would prove devastating for van Meegeren.

Is it a Vermeer or a van Meegeren? An "authentic" Vermeer painting, The Letter.

When the fortunes of the Third Reich and Hermann Göring took their final tumble in a Berlin bunker at the end of the war, there began a bizarre sequence of events that exposed van Meegeren's second career. After the Allied investigators discovered *Christ and the Adulteress* among Göring's plundered art collection and traced it back to van Meegeren, the Dutch artist was brought before a war tribunal on charges of collusion with the Nazis. Engaging in commerce with the aggressors of Europe was more than frowned upon, and the charge of collusion carried the penalty of death by hanging. Faced with so grim a prospect, the shaken van Meegeren was left with no other choice but to reveal that he had forged the Göring Vermeer. This defense would change the grave collusion charge to the almost laudable act of defrauding the enemy. There was only one problem: the court did not believe van Meegeren's seemingly incredible claim.

In an attempt to clear himself of charges of collusion, van Meegeren gave police a demonstration of his forging talents.

Since all of van Meegeren's fakes had been authenticated, experts, not surprisingly, denied that such exquisite forgery was possible. As a result, the court was ready to rule van Meegeren guilty of collusion. The now terrified artist offered to prove his claim by painting a "Vermeer" right before the court's skeptical eyes. Police were assigned to observe van Meegeren in his studio as he went about creating another Vermeer.

Techniques of a Master Forger

As the police watched, van Meegeren gave a lesson in classical art forgery techniques. To get the cracked look of an old painting, the artist began with an authentic old painting already ravaged and cracked by time. Over the old painting van Meegeren would paint the new pic-

ture, which would retain the old cracks of the painting beneath. Van Meegeren was careful to choose only colors within the spectrum available in Vermeer's day to avoid tipping off any art historians, who would immediately spot the slightest speck of modern color. Van Meegeren was also meticulous in ensuring that the colors were formed of the same physical material that Vermeer would have used.

To these commonly known techniques, van Meegeren added two of his own that made his forgeries particularly difficult to detect. Physically, the process of hardening, which happens naturally to paint over time, is impossible to induce and must be faked. Other forgers have brushed a glue compound over their forged paintings to give them the correct hardened texture, but glue has always been easily detected by chemical analysis.

Instead of glue, van Meegeren applied a layer of artificial resin over the painting, which provided the necessary texture and passed the chemical test undetected.

Artistically, van Meegeren modeled the composition of his Vermeers on the works of Caravaggio. This was a particularly brilliant stroke for two reasons. First, since they believed Vermeer was greatly influenced by Caravaggio, historians were quick to authenticate van Meegeren's work because it supported their own theories. Second, by closely following the composition of a great master, van Meegeren got around the problem of classical composition, a difficult element for modern artists to replicate. These two key elements, one artistic and one physical, had discouraged any doubts about van Meegeren's fakes.

The new Vermeer amazed the tribunal, convincing them that the Göring painting was a fake, and all charges of collusion were dropped. However, van Meegeren was not free of the courtroom altogether; civil authorities had the artist arrested and charged with fraud for his other forgeries. The Dutchman was convicted of fraud but given the light sentence of only a year in prison. Van Meegeren, worn out by his legal ordeals, died in his prison cell from a heart attack.

All the way to the end, van Meegeren claimed that his main goal was to embarrass the art aristocracy by revealing how little they actually knew about the work artists do. In large part he succeeded. No fewer than ten Vermeers and eight other forgeries are known to be van Meegeren fakes. No one knows how many other of his forgeries grace the walls of museums and mansions throughout the world.

Britain's Celebrity Forger

More than thirty years after van Meegeren, in the freewheeling 1970s, the twentieth century's other noted forger, Tom Keating of England, also claimed to be motivated by scorn of big-time art dealing and critics. Keating specialized in forging Samuel Palmer drawings, which sold for fifteen thousand to thirty thousand dollars each. The take per forgery was far less than van Meegeren got for a faux Vermeer, but Keating relied on volume: some estimate that Keating sold as many as two thousand fakes. Since no one knows how many drawings Palmer actually did, few challenged the flood of these high-quality works hitting the market. Furthermore, more people than just the forger were turning a buck trading in the forged art.

Keating, a gifted cockney artist, first tried mimicking Palmer as a way to relax in the evenings. When his wife remarked on how authentic the drawings looked, Keating took steps to make the forgeries

Hans van Meegeren's Vermeer Forgeries

Supper at Emmaus	(his first, and often considered his best)
Young Christ	
Christ and the Adulteress	(painting sold to Nazi Herman Göring)
The Washing of Christ's Feet	
Jesus in the Temple	(painted for tribunal to prove he was a forger)

even more believable. The forger gathered unused pages from Victorian photo albums, old diaries, writing papers, and even ledgers so that the paper he worked on would be the right age. The most elegant and famous of Keating's fakes, *Stepham Barn*, is a work Samuel Palmer himself would have been proud of.

Keating eventually revealed himself in the British press through an art journalist who had sought him out in order to find the source of all the new Palmers. Keating admitted directly that he had forged the pieces and took particular pleasure in implicating dealers and authenticators all over Europe who had dealt in art that they must have suspected was forged but for which they had set aside scruples to go on collecting fat fees and commissions as the forgeries circulated through the art world. The art commerce world was stung and many reputations were destroyed in the scandal, while Keating was able to escape the legal system with just a hand slap. Now famous and even popular in England, Keating ended up with his own show on the BBC. He followed up his moment in the limelight by publishing an autobiography called *The Fake's Progress*. The book, naturally, was ghostwritten.

The Art of the Steal

Of course, if a person is not gifted with a steady hand and an eye for color, forgery is out of the question. But stealing art is a time-proven occupation carried on by nations and private citizens alike. Long before the Nazis, art was carried away as plunder by the conquering armies of expanding empires including the French, British, and Romans. When the Roman conqueror Marcellus brought wagon loads of Greek art back to Rome from the conquered city of Syracuse earlier than 200 B.C., he ignited his hometown's interest in art and set a precedent for plundering treasures more elegant than mere gold and slaves. That the treasures of ancient Egypt and Greece are spread across the world speaks of the practice of plundering art as the spoils of war.

Of course, stealing art is not an occupation limited to conquering armies—a great many private individuals have found the endeavor quite lucrative. In fact, art theft and smuggling are so prevalent today that crime experts say the international trade in stolen art is second only to drug smuggling in terms of volume and value.

For the art thief, there are basically two problems. The first problem, obviously, is the theft itself, although stealing art is often quite easy. The second problem is unloading the stolen art in a market seemingly obsessed with proof of authenticity and ownership. One simple rule for the art thief is this: the more well known and valuable the object, the more difficult it will be to smuggle and sell it.

The thieves who succeed at art theft generally stick to lesser works of the popular old masters, because while these works are not as valuable as a van Gogh self-portrait, for example, they attract less attention and still bring respectable money. Art is also rarely as well protected as money in the bank; people like to show off their possessions and this makes the works vulnerable.

The Manor House Gang

In the 1960s, France was enjoying good economic times, and prosperity is always good news for art thieves. When there is plenty of money, the art market comes alive with people looking to buy art as a hedge against future bad times and to display their treasures in their easily robbed homes. In short, there were plenty of people to sell to and steal from. In these years there was an epidemic of mansion robberies throughout the country, which had police and insurance companies scurrying in all directions at once.

The king of the house robbers was a man as unlikely in appearance as can be imagined, but his band of thieves, dubbed the Manor House Gang, sacked more than a hundred mansions and châteaus in a two-year spree that was cut short in 1964. Dr. Xavier Richier, the leader of this band

than usual. Richier personally stole a Gothic tapestry depicting St. Gervais and Protais from the St. Julian Cathedral in Le Mans and sold it to a crooked dealer he had often used before. But when the dealer decided the piece was too hot to handle, he mailed it back to the church in

> "Art theft is a two-billion-dollar-a-year business in the form of burglaries, gallery thefts, and the looting of archeological sites."
>
> Constance Lowenthal, International Foundation for Art Research, 1992

of weekend robbers, was a small, bespectacled physician who lived in a modest house on a modest salary and ordinarily spent his time attending to the lungs and livers of the coal miners of Livien.

Richier's methods were simple but effective: he would keep an eye on selected country estates until he was certain that the residents were away, smash his way in through a door or window, and load the valuables into a waiting car, van, or truck. In addition to paintings and sculpture, the Manor House Gang stole tapestries, Louis XIV and XV tables and chairs, Napoleonic vases, and practically anything else worth taking, with the total value of all stolen goods estimated at $6.5 million. Richier funneled the stolen works to contacts in America; because the items were not famous enough to garner international attention when stolen, American art dealers bought the merchandise without ever suspecting it had been secured through illegitimate means.

The Manor House Gang was never caught in the act and never left a usable clue at a crime scene. They were brought down, however, when Richier succumbed to the temptation to go for a bigger prize

hopes of ending the matter. The police traced the packaging back to the dealer, and the dealer fingered Richier.

The police were skeptical at first that this quiet man could be the notorious thief. Their skepticism evaporated, however, when they went to Richier's house and found art and antiques stacked to the ceiling in every room, including the attic. The doctor was bound for jail. Of the nearly seven million dollars' worth of art stolen by Richier and his gang, far less than a third has ever been recovered. Most likely, Richier would never have been caught had he resisted the rare and famous tapestry and stuck to the lucrative trade in lesser-known works.

The Great English Art Theft

An even more unlikely-looking art thief than Dr. Richier was portly Kempton Bunton of Birmingham, England, who carried out the most famous art rip-off England has ever known.

In 1961, the retired Bunton was living on £8 a week, and his only pleasure was watching television. Crotchety and eccentric, Bunton had simmered for years in

not only the guards who patrolled the building but also the elaborate system of infrared beams that should have raised an alarm when anyone entered the building at night. Police naturally suspected the culprit was a master thief but were puzzled over why such a pro would steal a piece that was so famous it would be nearly impossible to sell and absolutely impossible to ever display. The thief's aims became clear when a letter arrived at the Reuters news agency ten days after the theft, demand-

Bunton, Kempton Bunton. The English public expected a James Bond type to emerge as the thief of Goya's Duke of Wellington *(shown below). The portly Bunton took the painting as a protest and to help charity.*

anger over the fact that the government did not exempt pensioners such as himself from the monthly license fee levied for BBC television service. The old man's anger exploded when he read that the government was paying £140,000 to keep a Goya portrait of the Duke of Wellington (a man Bunton had never heard of) from leaving British soil. The old pensioner decided that he would get even.

On the morning of August 21, 1961, the nation was shocked to learn that the most famous painting in England had been stolen from the National Gallery in the heart of London. Goya's *Duke of Wellington* had been snatched from its place in the front gallery by a thief able to confound

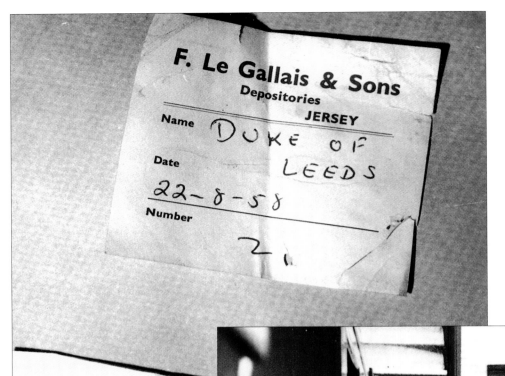

ing £140,000 be donated to charity and amnesty be granted to the thief in exchange for the stolen Goya. The police refused to cooperate with the ransom request, and a waiting game played out torturously over the next four years. The thief sent five letters demanding money be paid to charity but no action was taken on any of them. The public buzzed with speculation about the painting's whereabouts and who the Robin Hood thief might be. In the film *Dr. No*, James Bond encounters the *Duke of Wellington* hanging

TOP: *To prove he was the real crook, Bunton sent a label known to have been attached to the Goya along with a letter to a British news agency stating his demands.*

BOTTOM: *Police inspect the window in a National Gallery men's room where the Goya thief entered and exited the building. Some doubt that Kempton Bunton, a slightly disabled pensioner, could have negotiated the opening.*

in the extravagant hideout of his villainous antagonist, but in reality, the painting was still at large.

Tiring of the waiting game, Bunton was eventually deceived by a London newspaper into believing that at least a small amount of money would make its way to charity if he returned the painting. Bunton had a young man deposit a package with the painting hidden inside at the baggage office of the New Street Station in Birmingham. The police were informed of the painting's location, and they were able to recover the missing picture without its frame but still in good condition. After nearly four years the painting was returned to the gallery, but it would be a few more months before the thief revealed himself.

At sixty-one years of age and 250 pounds (113.5kg), Kempton Bunton was so unlikely a suspect that the police did not at first believe him when he tried to turn himself in. Bunton had blurted out his evil deed over pints of beer in a pub and came to the police of his own volition to prevent anyone from collecting a reward for turning him in. To prove to the police that he was indeed the culprit, Bunton produced the tablet on which he had written the demand letters and explained over and over how he had pulled off the theft. For a first-time thief, Bunton had pulled off a pretty masterful job.

The first thing Bunton had done was case the museum and start up conversations with the guards. In their apparently idle chatter with the old guy, the guards spilled the fact that security was lax in the wee hours when the electronic security was turned off for the cleaning crews. Nor, at that time of the morning, were the guards as meticulous in making their rounds. Days before the theft, Bunton disabled the latches of a restroom window for easy access to the building. When he observed over the following days that no one noticed the unlocked window, he proceeded with his simple plan.

Early in the morning, Bunton took a ladder from a nearby construction site to climb to the prepared window. He padded through the museum just ahead of the cleaning crews as soon as the infrared beams were shut off. Alone in the gallery, he snatched the painting and returned to the restroom, where he lowered the Goya by rope to the ground below. He returned to his home in northern England with the painting wrapped up under his arm, and nobody suspected the portly old pensioner had made off with the *Duke of Wellington*. It was that easy.

Edvard Munch's The Scream *(1893) was eventually recovered from thieves.*

Stolen Scream

Just before the Winter Olympics of 1994, Norway's most famous painting, *The Scream* (1893) by Edvard Munch, was stolen from Oslo's National Museum of Art. The thieves simply used a ladder to climb to a window, which they broke to get at the painting. They were in the museum for less than a minute—just enough time to make off with the painting and leave a note thanking the museum "for the poor security." An anti-abortion group claimed to have the painting and demanded the government broadcast an anti-abortion film titled *Silent Scream*. Although the painting was eventually recovered, the actual motives of the thieves remain unclear.

Like many other notorious thieves, Bunton became a celebrity in England as his trial date neared. After brief deliberation, the jury decided to find Bunton guilty only of stealing the picture frame, which was never recovered. The jury reasoned that since Bunton never intended to keep the Goya, he was not technically guilty of theft. The jury's decision tied the hands of the less sympathetic judge, who could sentence Bunton to only three months in prison.

Big Jobs by the Pros

Bunton's theft illustrates the inherent problem involved in stealing famous art: the police can afford patience because they know that the thief will have a very hard time unloading such a hot item. In some of the biggest jobs ever done, this problem has proved fatal; in others it has actually been used to clever advantage.

In January 1976, several robbers hit the Papal Palace in Avignon, France, where more than two hundred Picassos were on display. After closing time, two of the robbers, who had been hiding inside, jumped and pistol-whipped the guards one at a time until all were subdued. The thieves then opened the doors for their accomplices and quickly spirited away one hundred eighteen of the more important works, pulling off the biggest art robbery the world had ever seen.

As in the British Goya case, the police were patient in looking for leads. The thieves tested the waters looking for buyers and felt lucky when they met a man who said he had a connection in the American mob who might want to buy the whole lot. They settled on a price and

Infallible planning. The Papal Palace at Avignon, France, was raided by thieves, who carried off a staggering number of Picassos that were on temporary display. Their sin was undone when they tried to sell the entire collection to the police.

set up a meeting not far from where the paintings were stolen. But when the thieves showed up to the meeting, they learned it was a setup: the buyers were the police, and the gang and all the paintings were swiftly rounded up.

As already mentioned, the act of stealing famous art has never been the main problem. On April 14, 1991, someone broke into the Van Gogh Museum in Amsterdam and quickly grabbed twenty paintings valued at $500 million. The

The Biggest Art Theft In History

The biggest art rip-off in history began in the wee hours of March 18, 1990, as Boston's annual Saint Patrick's Day festivities wound down. At the Isabella Stewart Gardner Museum, the front doorbell rang, and the desk guard charged with watching the elaborate electronic surveillance system saw two policemen on the television monitor. When the guard asked the police over the intercom what they wanted, the

What, me nervous? An Isabella Gardner Museum security man looks understandably insecure. Professional thieves waylaid his colleagues and made off with $200 million in masterpieces—all uninsured.

night erupted with alarms as police flooded the Rembrandtplatz to begin the investigation just minutes after the thieves escaped. But before the news could spread that the paintings were gone, the van Goghs were discovered in an abandoned car near the museum. Had the thief despaired over the chances of unloading the art? Was there some crazy mix-up?

The paintings were gone from the museum for a total of only thirty-five minutes. To this day, no one knows why the thief abandoned them so quickly, but he or she could have conducted the most lucrative art heist ever.

cops replied that they were responding to a report of a disturbance and needed to check out the premises. The guard buzzed them in.

Once inside, the policemen started chatting amiably with the desk guard and asked him to summon the only other guard in the museum who was patrolling the floors. The mood swiftly changed, however, when one of the cops said he recognized the desk guard as a wanted criminal. In a flash, both museum guards were turned to the wall and handcuffed. Not until that moment did either guard suspect the cops might be impostors.

One of the phony cops immediately went to the electronics room to shut down the video recorders and remove the tapes that had been recording the evening's activities. Next, the guards were wrapped in duct tape; eyes, ears, mouth, hands, arms, legs, and feet were heavily taped to make observation and movement impossible. The guards were then handcuffed to heating pipes at opposite ends of the basement hallway, where they were to spend the rest of the night.

Once the guards and security cameras had been dealt with, the rest of the band of thieves were admitted into the building, where they moved precisely through the twenty-five-room, four-story gallery to get at their specifically chosen prey.

In the room of seventeenth-century paintings, the thieves used screwdrivers and chisels to pull Rembrandt's *Storm on the Sea of Galilee* (one of the artist's rare sea subjects) and *Lady and Gentleman in Black* from the wall and out of their frames. They ignored other great works as they moved from room to room executing a detailed plan. In addition to the Rembrandts, the targeted paintings were:

Jan Vermeer's *The Concert*

Govaert Flinck's *Landscape with an Obelisk*

Rembrandt's *Portrait of the Artist as a Young Man*

Edgar Degas' *La Sortie du Passage* and four other watercolors

Édouard Manet's *Chez Tortoni*

The thieves ignored other nearby works by Michelangelo, John Singer Sargent, and Whistler, all of which could have easily been added to the haul. In fact, they left a Rembrandt self-portrait on the floor for no apparent reason other than it was not on their very specific list. While they eschewed other masterworks, the thieves did take two small items apparently on impulse—a small Shang Dynasty Chinese vase and a decorative eagle removed from the staff of a Napoleonic battle flag.

In the morning, the daytime security guards called the real police, and the damage was assessed. A total of $200 million in art had been stolen in the form of the eleven paintings and the vase. (The Napoleonic eagle was of such minor consequence that it was days before it was even missed. Investigators suspect that it and the vase were taken as souvenirs.) For the museum, the horror was made even more profound by the fact that none of the works in the gallery was insured, at the behest of the late benefactor, Isabella Gardner. The museum had relied on its expensive security system, which had failed miserably.

To this day, none of the paintings has been recovered, despite a million-dollar reward. Normally, police and investigators are optimistic that such famous works will be recovered—they usually turn up within seven years—but in this case, there is reason for pessimism.

The precision of the thieves indicates that they were supreme professionals. The fact that they took only specific works indicates they may have been working from a list provided for them—they cared nothing about art or its value, but were just doing a job, most likely for a flat rate. It is not difficult to further conclude that the sale to the final owner and the means of getting the stolen art to him or her were also carefully planned. Perhaps these works of Rembrandt and Degas already adorn the walls of a private gallery out of the reach of international law.

OPPOSITE: *Rembrandt's* Storm on the Sea of Galilee, *which was stolen from the Isabella Stewart Gardner Museum.*

A da Vinci to Call One's Own   81

The grand prize. Leonardo da Vinci's Mona Lisa, *the most famous painting in the world, spent twenty minutes under Vincenzo Perugia's smock and two years hidden in his room. Paris was scandalized by the theft.*

The Greatest Art Coup of All Time: The *Mona Lisa*

While the Gardner robbery is the biggest art job in history in terms of money, it may not be the greatest in terms of what was stolen and how the theft was exploited. Seventy-nine years before the Gardner theft, someone dared to steal the most famous painting in the world and sell it six times over. The coup was masterminded by a rare individual with the highly refined talents of the con artist.

Argentinean Eduardo de Valfierno, "the Marques" as he allowed himself to be called, entered the game of selling art forgeries when he was left without a fortune as the younger son of an aristocrat. In order to stave off poverty and, even worse, real work, Valfierno at first supported himself by selling off his own elegant art and antiques to friends and contacts in the upper class. When his own possessions ran out, the young man decided that rather than take on the job of a soldier, diplomat, or clergyman, he would continue as a salesman of apparently valuable items that were actually forged. It was Valfierno's luck to happen upon Yves Chaudron, a talented art restorer and reproductionist who was also looking for a more lucrative life.

Both Chaudron and Valfierno decided that forged Spanish masters were the route to go, and Chaudron began turning out fake Murillos with a flare for forgery that was very rare indeed. Using the guise that these paintings had just come on the market from a friend, or by just "helpfully" guiding a visitor to a "reputable" dealer, Valfierno quickly mastered the life of the charlatan and was never caught. The richest resource for the charmer to mine was to be found among the wealthy widows of South America, who were anxious to donate an original Murillo to the Church in the name of their dearly departed. Valfierno and Chaudron turned out so many Murillos that their operation became known as the Murillo factory. One of their fakes actually made it into the Vatican collection, where it was not exposed as a fake for decades.

Picasso Implicated

At one point during the height of the hysteria over the theft of the *Mona Lisa*, the police and the public thought they had their men. A thief who had stolen small items from the Louvre fingered the poet Guillaume Apollinaire and his friend, a young Spanish artist named Pablo Picasso. The men were indeed found in possession of busts stolen from the Louvre and were hauled in for questioning in the *Mona Lisa* case. Hoping to get off the hook, Picasso denied even knowing his close friend Apollinaire, who was in danger of taking the fall for the big theft. Both men were eventually cleared and released. To his dying day, Picasso considered his betrayal of his friend the darkest moment of his life.

Sometime after the turn of the century, Valfierno became bored with the game in Argentina and decided to move to Europe. Chaudron decided to remain behind to continue the work he was so good at, only without so brilliant a front man, the reclusive Chaudron could only look forward to declining sales. Even though their partnership was at an end, the two men parted friends when Valfierno sailed to France.

In 1910, Valfierno came upon his grandest scheme ever. While in Paris, he read about the difficulty of security at the immense Louvre, where petty thefts had become an ongoing problem. Valfierno also noted that many of the great paintings were being put in protective shadow boxes, the glass of which protected the works from the occasional vandal. In short, the museum was vulnerable, and a lot of legitimate activity surrounded the paintings as they were taken from display to be boxed and photographed. Valfierno knew that there was an opportunity for him within the museum.

It is not known for how long the clever mind turned over these bits of information before striking on the final plan. Perhaps the scheme became complete when Valfierno's old friend and accomplice, Chaudron, surfaced in Paris after business in Argentina had petered out. At some point,

Valfierno shared with Chaudron the idea of a lifetime and they set about bringing it to reality.

Pablo Picasso, world-famous artist and onetime suspect in the Mona Lisa *robbery.*

Stealing the *Mona Lisa*

Early in the morning on August 21, 1911, three men passed their last uncomfortable hours of the night crammed in a storage closet in the Louvre. It was a Monday morning, and Mondays were set aside for the cleaning and maintenance of the museum's 225 rooms and five miles (8km) of corridors. In the morning light, workers arrived dressed in the long white blouses that were issued by the museum. None of the workers noticed Vincenzo Peruggia and his two accomplices emerge from the storage room door, or if they did, they thought nothing of it because all three men wore the same white blouses as the regular workers.

When three men in white blouses took the *Mona Lisa* from its place on the wall in the Salon Carre and carried it away inside its shadow box, not a challenge was spo-

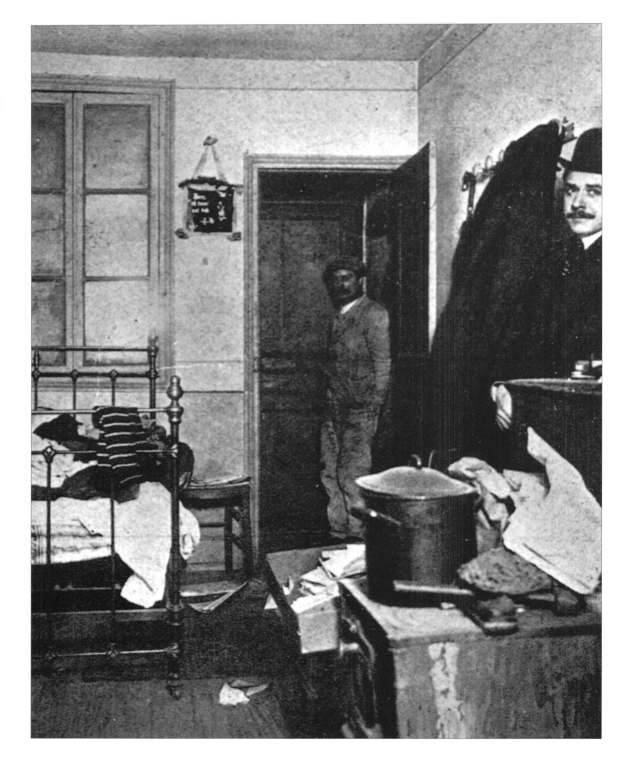

Police revisited Peruggia's Paris room where they had interviewed him shortly after the theft and concluded he was not involved. The Italian carpenter fashioned a false panel to hide the painting in the wall.

ken—such an activity was common in the museum. The thief Peruggia and his men got the painting to a stairwell to remove the protective box; Peruggia had no problem dealing with the box because he was the carpenter who had made it for the museum. Now the bulky mass was reduced to only the masterpiece, which had been painted by Leonardo da Vinci on a sheet of white poplar wood. Peruggia tucked the famous painting under his blouse and casually stepped back onto the floor of the museum.

At the door, the thieves had a few tense moments while waiting for the guard to be distracted. When he was, Peruggia strolled right out the door and into the Parisian sunshine. The *Mona Lisa* was stolen; the greatest coup in the history of art theft had just been pulled off. Peruggia made it back to his apartment unchallenged. Shockingly, it was twenty-seven hours before anyone at the Louvre realized that the most famous painting in the world was really gone.

The Parisian public and press went nuts. First, it was widely believed and hoped that the disappearance was just a hoax and the *Mona Lisa* would soon be returned. As the days passed and the massive police investigation turned up nothing, ridicule was heaped on the police and the men charged with security at the Louvre. The *Paris Journal* ran the following flyer and urged readers to post copies of it around the Louvre:

> In the interest of Art
> And for the Safeguarding of the Precious Objects
> THE PUBLIC
> Is requested to Be Good Enough to
> WAKE THE GUARDS
> If they are found to be Asleep.

L'Illustation offered forty thousand francs for the return of the painting, no questions asked. But days, weeks, and finally months passed with nothing turning up but false rumors and crackpot confessions to aid the police.

Nothing was seen of the *Mona Lisa* for two years, and its disappearance was a topic never far from the city's conscience. But when Peruggia turned up two years after the robbery in Italy and foolishly tried to sell the painting to the Uffizi Gallery in Florence, he and the painting were seized. At his trial, the Italian Peruggia claimed that he had acted alone and in anger because he believed that the French, whom he despised, had no right to own an Italian masterpiece. The excitable and slightly crazy Peruggia was sentenced to prison; the painting was returned to its home in France; and most everyone thought that was the end of the story.

The Rest of the Story

The dogged historical research of a man named Seymour V. Reit uncovered the deeper truth about the robbery, including the involvement of Valfierno, of which the authorities were unaware. According to Reit, Valfierno began his scheme months before the painting was taken. First, Valfierno put Chaudron to work painting six high-quality reproductions of the *Mona Lisa*. While Chaudron went about this task, Valfierno picked Peruggia, whom he learned had worked in the Louvre, to do the actual stealing. The Marques promised the intense Peruggia some money up front and more money after he sold the stolen painting. Valfierno told Peruggia nothing about the six copies he was having made. In fact, Valfierno told Peruggia nothing of

the real plot, nor did he tell him his real name or even where he could be reached. All Peruggia knew was that this high-class character was to pay him to steal the *Mona Lisa*.

Valfierno crossed the Atlantic to re-sume connections with customers and op-eratives in North and South America. He carefully picked the most unscrupulous of the wealthy buyers of the world's art. The *Mona Lisa* was mentioned. Overtures were carefully made as to who might be interested in buying such a hot item should it become available. Six buyers were lined up—unknown to one another—each willing to pay $300,000 to own a painting they could never show. Five of the buyers were in the United States, one in Brazil. By setting up the sale in advance, Valfierno was able to sidestep questions about authenticity—surely the man who could predict that the painting was to disappear would have the actual item. With the sting set up, Valfierno returned to France.

When Chaudron completed the fakes, Valfierno sent them across the ocean. Since he did this before the theft, customs officials passed the fakes through with no problem; they allowed scores of fakes through their borders on a daily basis, and there was nothing suspicious about a fake *Mona Lisa*.

With the stage set, Valfierno sent Peruggia into action. Once Peruggia and his men had completed the theft, Valfierno visited Peruggia to confirm that he had the painting and to pay him for his trouble. The Marques instructed the carpenter to stash the painting and await further instructions and more money. Peruggia dutifully obeyed, but the further instructions never came.

The Sting

Valfierno decided to catch a steamer to the Americas so that he could arrive with full drama after the theft to close the deals. All six buyers happily paid for their Chaudron fakes and took them away to whatever secret place they planned to keep the *Mona Lisa* and revel in their good fortune and cleverness. When the money changed hands, the crime became essentially perfect. The buyers of the fakes became accomplices in the crime and would never

dare to go public. In addition, Valfierno knew that once the real painting came to light, none of the megalomaniac buyers would want anyone to know they had been such a dupe and so would keep silent. Even if one of the buyers was able to locate Valfierno, it was not beyond his powers of persuasion to convince the angry buyer that he indeed had the real *Mona Lisa* and the Louvre had cooked up the whole story about Peruggia just to save face. If there was a fake it was hanging in the Louvre! This ploy had been used and had worked before. On the other side of the Atlantic, should Peruggia get cold feet, he would not be able to either name or find Valfierno.

Valfierno probably planned to pay Peruggia, take the *Mona Lisa* from him, and find a way to return it to the Louvre. Such a move would have closed the case with the elegant symmetry that would have appealed to a man like Valfierno, but somewhere along the line he let this part of the plan slip away. Left hanging in the wind, Peruggia made the Florence move on his own and, after his sloppy sales attempt at the Uffizi, was easily apprehended. As for why Peruggia claimed that he had acted alone, Reit believes—with good reason—that the Italian both enjoyed his burst of celebrity and, like the dupes in the Americas, probably was not eager to reveal that he had been made a fool.

Valfierno was able to combine forgery, theft, and the clever ways of the con artist to pull off the perfect crime. In the end, the *Mona Lisa* ended up in the Louvre; Peruggia ended up briefly in prison; Chaudron retired in great comfort; and Valfierno traveled the world in style, perhaps dreaming up new schemes no one has yet been clever enough to unravel.

OPPOSITE: *Passionate thief. Peruggia claimed he stole the da Vinci masterpiece because it belonged in Italy and could not bear to see it in a French museum. But Peruggia was covering up the fact that he had himself been duped by a master con man.*

Chapter

THE STAR OF INDIA

This remarkably beautiful and ancient gem weighs 563.35 carats, and it is said to be the largest cut sapphire in the world.

CEYLON
The Gift of
the late John Pierpont Morgan

This uniquely beautiful star ruby which weighs 100 carats, is rumored to be the largest and finest star ruby in the world.

BURMA
The Gift of
Mrs. George Bowen de Long

CORUNDUM GEMS

THE REALLY GOOD STUFF

Four

Jewels. Gold. The good stuff. Of all professional thieves, the most elite are the cat burglars who glide silently over fences and through windows into the most intimate and protected reaches of their victims' worlds wholly undetected. At any one time there are probably fewer than two dozen first-rate jewel thieves plying their trade around the globe; the number can only be guessed at because jewel thieves are the most elusive and tight-lipped of all criminals. They are generally superb athletes, masters of their craft, and nightmares for the police, who often know the names of particular cat burglars and their modes of operation but are rarely able to prove what they know. What is known about these thieves comes from the mouths of the very few who have talked.

House Invaders

Contrary to the image many of us have of the burglar creeping through a mansion's rooms while the victims sleep, one of the world's most notorious jewel thieves preferred working in broad daylight. Albie Baker started as a small-time thief in New York City during the Depression and graduated, pretty much on his own, to big-time jewel burglary. Baker's approach was bold and effective enough to rack up millions of dollars in jewel thefts in the United States and Europe.

The first step for any thief, naturally, is to stake out a hunting ground and learn the lay of the land. When Baker moved in on a new community, he had a regular routine for ferreting out the best prospects for burglarizing, starting with the local newspaper. In addition to carefully comb-ing the society columns—as all jewel thieves do—Baker regularly perused the pages of *Lloyd's Registry of Yachts*, *Poor's Almanac*, *Town and Country*, *Vogue*, and *Harper's Bazaar* looking for victims. Eschewing the anonymity and stealth most burglars prefer, Baker used his college-boy good looks, nice clothes, and classy car to infiltrate the highest stratum of society in order to better stalk his prey. When Baker came to town, he played tennis in the best clubs and became a regular at the swankest watering holes of the rich, where he could stealthily observe his next victims like a lion selecting the fattest, most vulnerable zebra.

Once he had picked his marks, Baker would case their neighborhoods by day, when police and security guards would think nothing of a handsome, sharply dressed young man in an expensive, sporty car coming and going amid all the other traffic of the day. Over the course of a few weeks, Baker would learn and mentally note who was home, who was gone, and whose maids were off at any given time or day. Once all these observations had been made, Baker was ready.

In January 1940, early in his career, Baker followed these precise procedures in Miami before making his move against the Williams mansion in the city's best neighborhood. Baker had learned that the couple had no children, that they were both away from their house most afternoons, and that the maid got one weekday off on a regular basis. Dressed with his usual casual elegance and at the wheel of his sports car, Baker drove to the Williams home in midafternoon, parked near the house, and strode purposefully up the driveway. To any random observer, he was just a friendly caller.

At the back door, Baker knocked loudly to make sure nobody was home and to allay suspicion should a neighbor happen to be looking out a window. When, as expected, no one came to the door, Baker jimmied it open with a small lever and went inside the house calling out a friendly greeting; if someone was at home and responded, he could act as though he had mistakenly come to the wrong house and make his getaway. When no one answered, Baker swiftly ran from room to room in the house to be sure once and for all that he was alone. Next, a quick search of the master bedroom was usually all that was required to uncover any jewel cases. A few minutes after entering the house, Baker left with $100,000 worth of jewelry.

Baker always left the scene with the same confident innocence he had displayed while entering. The thief would either stride back down the driveway to his car or, even more boldly, leave by the front door smiling and waving to the interior of the house as though ending a pleasant visit with the inhabitants. Baker had three main reasons for striking in daylight: the activity of strangers is less suspicious; most police department burglary squads don't go on duty until four o'clock in the afternoon; and most women don't wear many jewels during the daytime, which means there will be more behind at home to steal.

Although Baker had many successes stealing in this way, he was caught more than once—one time while in the act—

The stereotypically thuggish jewel thief. In fact, these most elite of thieves rarely use flashlights, which draw too much attention, and almost never carry guns. They rely instead on stealth, speed, and intelligence.

and spent many years of his life in prison. Furthermore, as illustrious as Baker was, he does not typify the professional jewel thief. More typical of the profession is Peter Salerno, who started his career in the 1960s and went on to successfully terrorize the rich for decades.

The Thief's Thief

Peter Salerno learned the jewel thief's trade from an established professional in the early 1960s. Standing five feet seven inches (1.7m) tall and weighing two hundred pounds (90.8kg), without an ounce of fat, Salerno, who could run for hours and easily climb any wall or rope, was physically perfect for the job. His teacher, Frank Bova, had learned how to steal while he was a soldier; Bova had been rigorously trained in the craft of stealing documents from the Nazis. Bova and Salerno worked together for a while until Salerno was ready to go out on his own and Bova was ready to retire from the thieving life, having never been captured.

A Jewel Thief on the Harmlessness of His Profession

"They're gonna recover what I'm taking as a luxury from them temporarily. They don't need [diamonds] to live. You could live without diamonds."

Peter Salerno, master jewel thief

The techniques Salerno developed differed from Baker's in many ways. In scouting for scores, Salerno educated himself about real estate, beginning with the basic lesson that the wealthiest people tend to live near water or golf courses or both. Salerno also became something of an expert about swimming pools, enabling him to tell with just a quick glance over a backyard wall how much a rich person had laid out to stay cool in the summer. The rule for identifying the best probable victims was simple—anyone who would pay lavish sums of money for a high-profile house and an extravagant pool would certainly be equally ostentatious when he or she bought jewelry. To Salerno, people who lived like kings were walking treasure troves begging to be robbed.

Once the victim was chosen, Salerno's modus operandi was consistent from job to job. He would hide his tools (a simple crowbar, penlight, and rope—never a gun) somewhere near the chosen target a few days before the robbery. In the early evening of the appointed day, Salerno would either park his car or be dropped off a few miles from his tools to avoid having a car parked near the crime scene, which could arouse suspicion or identify him. In fact, as a further precaution, Salerno often parked his car in a shopping center, where no notice would be taken of a vacant automobile. This taken care of, Salerno would sneak through the night on foot—sticking to forests whenever he could and being careful crossing roads to be sure no one saw him—until he had retrieved his tools and arrived at the targeted house.

At the fence or wall around the house, Salerno (and his accomplice, if he had one) would check for an electronic alarm system. If he found such an alarm, the accomplice would help him vault over the fence without ever touching it or disturbing the electronic sensor. Once in the yard, Salerno carefully approached the house, avoiding light and using any cover provided by trees or shrubs. Cautiously, Salerno would peep into every window to determine where all the residents and staff were.

Surprisingly, a professional like Salerno ordinarily strikes near the dinner hour, actually hoping that the residents will be home. If the residents are in their dining room or watching television in the den, chances are good that all their valuable jewelry is in the house with them. Furthermore, alarm systems are generally not turned on until later in the evening when the family and staff have ceased coming and going for the day. Once Salerno knew the location of everyone in the house, he would find the master bedroom and enter quietly through a window, being careful not to break it; the fewer signs he left behind, the better.

Professional jewel thieves strike the master bedroom because with remarkable regularity that is where people stash their jewels, preferring to keep them close by. Once inside the bedroom, Salerno would lock the hall door or jam a chair against it as an early-warning system; if anyone came to the door and rattled the knob trying to open it, Salerno would have plenty of time to escape back into the night before anyone could figure out what was going on. In case he had tripped a silent alarm, Salerno always limited his search of the master bedroom to four minutes, which was as fast as the police could possibly respond. Amazingly, these few minutes were always plenty of time to find the jewelry, no matter where it was hidden. Once he found the loot, Salerno used a pillowcase off the bed to carry away what he stole, and jewels were all he ever took. A pro does not mess with small antiques, art, or other valuable objects—only jewelry. Other than the missing pillow-

case, which would not be discovered for hours (and was Salerno's trademark), Salerno left no trace of his presence in order to delay detection and police investigation.

Salerno would then fly back into the night the way he had come. Not far from the house, he would bury his tools, and not far from where he did that, he would hide the jewels near a road to be picked up later. These precautions were taken to completely relieve Salerno's person of incriminating evidence. Should the police through some incredibly lucky stroke spot the thief and search him, there was nothing to prove he was doing anything more malicious than taking a stroll. Once back at his car and after making sure he was not being followed, Salerno would pick up the jewels and deliver them to a fence that same night. Again, this rapid transfer of the jewelry to the fence, who immediately broke them down, decreased the amount of time Salerno spent holding evidence that could be used against him. Such practices are what keep jewel thieves just beyond the reach of the police. Salerno pulled jobs like this several times a month and generally scored between $150,000 and $500,000 in jewelry per job.

The Vat 69 Score

At the height of his career, Salerno hit the owner of the Vat 69 liquor company in one of New York's wealthiest suburbs. He had to get past dogs, a high wall, and surveillance cameras inside the house to get at the goods. A master at his craft, Salerno took the job as a personal challenge and rose to the occasion by devising solutions to every obstacle.

Observing that the guard dogs were placed in a pen beside the house when there were guests, Salerno chose to strike on a night when the society columns reported there was to be a party at the mansion. The high wall would be no problem to an athlete like Salerno or his accomplice, but the cameras inside the house that kept all the windows under surveillance were a particularly tough obstacle. Several days in advance, Salerno picked the second-story window he would use for entry so that he could study the rotation of the camera in that room and get the precise dimensions of the window. Salerno saw that the pivoting camera passed its eye over the window every few seconds, which was not nearly enough time for two men to get through the window. It would take something special to beat the camera and get into the room.

On the night of the party, Salerno and his accomplice scaled the wall and perched there above the guests and servants just a short leap away from the window. Silently, Salerno jumped to the window, timing it so that the camera would be pointed away from him. Once inside the room, Salerno quickly unfurled a drawing of the window, which he held in front of him and the real window as his accomplice climbed in behind him. The camera's eye passed over the drawing, and the guard downstairs in charge of watching the TV monitors failed to notice the fingers holding up the fake window; Salerno had counted on the fact that whoever was watching the monitors had to watch several at a time and would never closely examine any of them. Salerno and his man went to the master bedroom and stole $750,000 worth of jewelry before repeating their false window trick to cover their escape.

Salerno is perhaps the most successful jewel thief on record because he managed to steal many millions of dollars in jewelry and was convicted only once when he was framed by former accomplices who were trying to get lighter sentences for themselves. However, to say that Salerno is the most successful thief *on record* does not mean as much as it may seem; very few of the greatest jewel thieves in the world are known to any official recordkeepers, and those who are known generally keep quiet.

Big Scores

Although there is little reason to believe that the methods of European cat burglars differ much from their colleagues in the rest of the world, jewel thieves on that continent have managed the biggest scores in the world and gotten away with them. European thieves are lucky because places like the French Riviera and such magnificent cities as Paris and Rome draw the greatest and richest names in the world, and therefore provide the most abundant hunting grounds to be found anywhere. It has been in Europe, twice since 1980, that members of Middle Eastern royalty have received very costly lessons at the hands of cat burglars.

One can only imagine the awe and delight felt by the intrepid burglars who on the night of September 18, 1992, found themselves in an "Aladdin's Cave" (so described by the usually staid *London Times*) of jewelry displayed in vanity cases and neat velvet boxes. The cave was actually Jordanian Princess Nirval's very upmarket flat in London's very, very upmarket Chapel Street. The princess, still very striking in her late forties, was something of a jewel collector, and the thief or thieves who forced the lock that night slipped out

of the building with seven million dollars' worth of rare jewelry.

The objects stolen were not the usual swag sought by thieves because a great deal of the jewels' value was in their historical significance. The most notable piece stolen was an engraved bracelet that Princess Nirval had purchased from the Duchess of Windsor's estate. Since the jewelry would have been very difficult to sell and would have lost a substantial amount of value if broken down, the police at first suspected that the burglary was an amateur job, but since the jewels have not turned up anywhere it is increasingly apparent the job was done by pros.

Twelve years before the London caper, a different Middle Eastern noble was victimized by thieves on the French Riviera.

Don't Fence Me In

What the papers report as the value of stolen jewelry in any given case is generally a far cry from what the thief actually receives. The value reported is generally the retail price, while the thief actually gets from his fence only a percentage of the wholesale value of the gems, which is half of retail. An experienced thief will get fifty percent of the wholesale value, which means he or she ends up with about a quarter of the value of the loot as reported in the newspapers.

Prince Abdul Aziz Ahmed al-Thani was relieved of sixteen million dollars in jewels, which must have been painful even to the son of the emir of oil-rich Qatar.

The thief in France picked a hot summer evening in July 1980 to strike at the prince's extensive villa in Cannes. The mysterious burglar must have observed that the lower-floor windows were kept open on hot nights for ventilation, because it was through one of those windows that he or she entered the house. The thief struck in the early evening after evidently seeing the prince and his wife move downstairs, leaving the second story of the home empty. Slipping past servants and a few guards, the thief helped him- or herself to the richest haul ever pulled in a house burglary before vanishing back into the warm night. Both the thief and the jewelry are still at large.

The Beachboy Caper

Brash Jack "Murph the Surf" Murphy (third from right) has always been the most famous of the Star of India thieves, but the quieter, high-living Alan Kuhn (to Murphy's right) was probably the planner of the heist.

Across the street from New York's Central Park, the American Museum of Natural History draws hundreds of visitors a day, as it has for decades. In the mid-1960s, the J.P. Morgan room, which houses an extensive display of exotic and valuable gems, was one of the least visited corners of the museum, probably because the quiet attraction of sparkling diamonds was only slight competition for the drama of an Indian diorama or the opportunity to view the world's largest known elephant tusk. However, in 1964 the Morgan room did receive a couple of frequent visitors— trim young men in their twenties whose skin still glowed with the sun of Florida and whose young eyes cast off hints of bleariness from all-night partying. The men were jewel thieves looking to pull off the world's most glamorous heist.

Suspicious Beginnings

They looked and lived like young gods. Alan Kuhn and Jack Murphy were famous in Miami among the beachboy crowd for their surfing, diving, and extravagant partying. To the Miami police, however, they

were more suspicious than famous since the men, Kuhn in particular, owned a two-masted sailing yacht, a powerful speed-boat called *The Missile*, a sumptuous apartment overlooking Biscayne Bay, and a new Cadillac convertible purchased with cash consisting of thousand-dollar bills—all at age twenty-six without a regular job or rich parents. The police smelled a rat but could prove nothing.

In 1964, while Lyndon Johnson was about to thrash Barry Goldwater and the Soviets still led the space race, Kuhn and convertible with what the FBI later described as two "stunning" young women and pointed the headlights north toward New York City. Once in the Big Apple, the young men set up in an expensive suite of rooms at the Cambridge Hotel on West 86th Street, and the word soon spread that suite 1803 was the place to be for nightly parties that rarely ended before the sun rose. But drinking and debauchery, for all their charms, were not the main things on the beachboys' minds; this was intended to be a business trip.

Murph the Surf on Being Arrested

"I was supposed to be on my way to Hawaii to surf," he said, lighting a cigar. "Now all this inconvenience has fouled the whole thing up."

Jack Murphy to The New York Times *(11/3/64).*
He spent most of the next twenty-two years behind bars.

Murphy (known to the beach crowd and later the world as "Murph the Surf") took a break from surfing the Florida coast to set sail for the Bahamas aboard Kuhn's yacht, *Virginia Dare*. The yacht was searched by police in Bimini after a $750,000 jewel heist, and even though nothing was found aboard, Kuhn and Murphy were ordered to leave. Later, when *Virginia Dare* anchored between Nassau and Andros, the yacht was raided again because police suspected the boys in a rash of jewel thefts at an Andros ho-tel. Again the boat was ordered to leave. Kuhn and Murphy and their girlfriends re-turned to Florida.

After spending the rest of the summer in the water, on the sand, or at the bar, Kuhn and Murphy hopped into Kuhn's

World's Biggest Jewel Heist

Murphy and Kuhn had come to New York to pull a house job, which for one reason or another fell through. The story that later circulated was that Kuhn got the idea to rob the American Museum of Natural History when he and his friends were browsing around New York trying to fig-ure out what they should do. After casing the museum for a few weeks and discov-ering its weak spots, Kuhn, Murphy, and a new accomplice they had met in Miami named Roger Clark solidified their plan to steal every gem in the J.P. Morgan room. They bought guidebooks to the museum and books about the collection as they went about mapping out their every move. If they succeeded, the job would make them the most daring and successful jewel thieves of all time, and they believed it would be a kick.

On the night of October 29, Kuhn pulled his big Cadillac into a parking space near the museum. Kuhn and Murphy left Clark in the car with a pair of binoculars and a walkie-talkie so that he could alert the thieves if the police drove up to the building. The two surfers walked calmly a few blocks to the museum parking lot, where they easily scaled the outer fence. In the darkness, they moved quickly to a second, ten-foot (3m) -high fence, on which iron bars tapered upward into sharp points. The thieves looped a rope over a crossbar so that they would have a foothold on either side of the spikes, and carefully climbed over the fence into the inner courtyards of the museum.

ways until they arrived at the wing that housed the J.P. Morgan room. Here, they scrambled up a fire escape to the fifth floor, crept out onto a ledge, and carefully scooted around the corner of the building until they were just above the room containing the gems. They fastened ropes to a fifth-floor window and silently descended to the fourth-floor windows of the Morgan room.

The keepers of the museum had provided the surfers with just enough help to make the theft feasible. The windows in the Morgan room, as Kuhn and Murphy had observed, were kept slightly open to allow air to circulate. Furthermore, the museum maintained only a few guards and had inexplicably disconnected the electronic alarm system designed specifically to protect the gems. Kuhn and

Lowbrow Amateurs

A bunch of New York construction workers were provided with an interesting break from work one cold November day in 1963 when their attention was drawn to a daring robbery taking place on a nearby sidewalk. A band of thieves dressed as cops enticed the driver of a station wagon delivering jewels to pull to the curb, rapidly abducted the guards in their car, and drove off. One of the thieves stayed behind to take the wheel of the station wagon full of diamonds. There was one problem: the getaway driver couldn't work a standard shift. The robber panicked and fled.

After hooting at the incompetent thief, the construction workers held a quick conference and decided to move the vehicle onto their work site and loot the million-dollar cargo themselves. They hid the diamonds all over the site and told police that the robbers had made off with the jewels. The police were fooled until the workers started bragging in local bars and word got back to the authorities. The workers were rounded up, and most of the gems were returned. Some of the missing gems, worth thousands of dollars, had been sold for almost nothing to smooth operators who had descended on the construction workers as word spread about the would-be theft.

The American Museum of Natural History is a huge building composed of multiple wings, which form the walls of canyonlike alleyways throughout the compound. Murphy and Kuhn moved confidently through these dark passage-

Murphy slid through an open window and went to work quickly cutting holes in the glass cases that held the gems. So far, the job had been a piece of cake.

Murphy and Kuhn had opened only three of the display cases when they were

spooked by a noise in the hall-way beyond the door that they feared might be a guard. Knowing they had already scooped up twenty-four of the most valuable jewels in the room, they decided to abandon the rest of the display cases and clear out. They slipped through the window and up the ropes to the ledge above, then retraced their steps to the fire escape and over the fences. Clark was waiting in the car and drove the thieves back to the Cambridge to survey the loot.

TOP: *At the American Museum of Natural History, police dust for fingerprints where eight huge gems should be. Police claimed that prints led them to Kuhn and Murphy, but it's more likely that a tip from an ungrateful bellhop broke the case.*

BOTTOM: *Big enough to choke an ox. The huge Star of India sapphire shines characteristically near an unidentified index finger. The other emeralds and aqua-marines pictured were also part of the beachboy haul.*

THE ☆ AK OF INDIA
This remarkably beautiful and ancient gem weighs 563.35 carats, and it is said to be the largest cut sapphire in the world.
CEYLON
The Gift of
the late John Pierpont Morgan

THE EDITH HAGGIN DE LONG STAR
This uniquely beautiful star ruby which weighs 100 carats, is repu-ted to be the lar est and finest star ruby in the
BURMA
The Gift of
Mrs. George Bowen de Long

On the table in their suite the thieves spread out before them an impressive array of diamonds, aquamarines, and emeralds. But the star of their new collection was the Star of India sapphire, the biggest sapphire in the world. The Star of India is so named because of the star-shaped glow that emanates from the center of the stone when it is held to the light; at 563 carats, this star shines from a sapphire the size of a golf ball. The Star of India made the Midnight Star sapphire (a measly 116.5 carats) and the De Long Star ruby (100.32 carats), both of which had also been pilfered by the surfers that night, look puny by comparison. But the thieves spent little time beholding their loot because they were in a hurry to get out of town.

Within twelve hours of the robbery, Murphy and Kuhn were flying back to Miami with the gems. More accurately, they were on the same plane as the gems, which were locked in a briefcase carried by Kuhn's unwitting new girlfriend, Janet

Flockiewicz. She had been handed the briefcase and told to behave as though she did not know Kuhn and Murphy. Flockiewicz did as she was told, hoping with all the naive optimism of a nineteen-year-old that Kuhn would deliver on his promise to be her boyfriend in eternal Miami luxury. As they winged their way toward Miami, Murphy and Kuhn felt like they had pulled off the perfect crime. The feeling was short-lived.

Wipeout

Within twenty-four hours of the heist, Murphy, Kuhn, and Clark were all in police custody. Although the police say that they had fingerprints from the museum and had suspected the beachboys from the start, it appears the Florida thieves were undone as much by their wild ways and generosity as anything else. A bellhop at the Cambridge alerted a local cop that the residents of suite 1803 were throwing money around like crazy and tipping the staff five dollars at a time. After the bellhop, one of the beneficiaries of these lavish tippers, reported them as suspicious, the police started staking out the room.

The cops nabbed Clark in the suite with two young women; the maps of the museum and books about the gems were enough evidence to indicate that the burglary had been planned there. Clark revealed the names and whereabouts of his cohorts, and a call to the Miami police did the rest of the New York police's work for them—or at least almost all the work, for the gems were still missing.

In exchange for leniency, Kuhn helped the New York police recover all the missing stones except for nine diamonds that had already been broken up and fenced. Kuhn flew with a New York prosecutor and police detectives back to Miami, where after a wild couple of days the stolen jewels were recovered in a bus-station rental locker. While in Miami, the police and Kuhn were forced to jump out twenty-foot (6m) windows, sneak through parking lots, and climb fences in order to escape the swarming press. At one point, an impressed Kuhn remarked to the prosecutor as they were climbing out a of window, "If you guys were burglars, I'd be out of business."

Kuhn, Murphy, and Clark were each sentenced to three consecutive one-year sentences. While they were being held in New York City, young women came to the police station or courthouse every day hoping to get a glimpse of Kuhn or Murph the Surf. The stories that emerged about the two of them—pistol-whipping Eva Gabor while robbing her in Florida or Murphy's beating of a New York Algonquin Hotel clerk—were largely ignored by their youthful fans. The thieves were released in 1966 after their sentences were reduced for good behavior.

For Murph the Surf, the good behavior ended when he hit the streets of Florida again. Whatever remained of his golden image was obliterated when he was convicted of the brutal robbery of a Miami socialite and the murder of two young women who may have been accomplices in an embezzlement scheme. In 1969, Murphy was sentenced to consecutive life sentences, and only an appeal for leniency from the jury kept him from being executed. At the age of forty-seven and still trim and athletic-looking, Murphy left prison on parole in 1986 with the vow to spend his life serving God and helping other prisoners.

Jack Murphy, after being held overnight at the police station while awaiting arraignment.

chapter

Five

ROBBERY WITH A SMILE

It takes a special kind of guts to rob a man eye-to-eye armed only with charm and a confidently delivered lie. Add to that kind of chutzpah an ability to assess and exploit various kinds of human weakness with cool precision, and you've got yourself a first-rate con artist—one of those cold souls who would rob the cup of a blind beggar with no more show of remorse than a cruel laugh. Con artists have probably been around since the invention of the lie, and despite their sociopathic ruthlessness, it is rare that their lives are not at least a little entertaining.

King of Sting. Victor Lustig, among his other cons, once got an Oklahoma sheriff to buy one of his phony money boxes; when the lawman hunted him down, Lustig offered to buy it back. The sheriff accepted the offer, only to end up in jail for trying to pass the counterfeit money Lustig had given him.

Master Con Artist

For a well-rounded education in the ways of the con man, one could do worse than study the life of Victor Lustig. Lustig, who often awarded himself the title the "Count," was originally from what are now the Czech and Slovakian Republics but rapidly became a citizen of the world. Using a variety of different aliases and ruses, Lustig embarked on an illustrious career, taking advantage of suckers on both sides of the Atlantic.

In the years around World War I, Lustig began his shadowy life as a professional gambler traveling back and forth over the ocean on the world's best luxury liners. The young European learned a great many things from legendary card-sharper Nicky Arnstein, including the art of picking a victim and the importance of finessing a mark to come right to him. Both talents served Lustig well when he disembarked in America to take up the life of the grifter full-time.

There's No Biz Like Show Biz

In the United States, one of Lustig's scams was suckering wealthy provincial theater lovers into believing that he was a Broadway producer. Lustig would travel with an aspiring starlet (also duped into believing he was a producer) until he picked a mark with the requisite amount of money and showbiz dreams. He would acquaint himself with the victim in the most casual of ways and wait patiently until the starlet eventually spilled the fact that Lustig was a big producer. The mark would start to question Lustig, who would remain evasive about the new play he was trying to finance. The mark usually pursued the subject until a reluctant Lustig would allow him to put up forty-nine percent—usually around forty thousand dollars. Cash in hand, Lustig would vanish, leaving a disillusioned starlet and an angry would-be co-producer in his wake.

The Money Box

One summer during the Roaring Twenties, even the best-heeled American vacationers lodging at the best hotel in Palm Beach, Florida, could not help but be impressed when Lustig arrived in a shining Rolls-Royce steered by a liveried driver. Never one to cut corners when grand style was required, the Count naturally set himself up in the finest suite available. His suave ways, European title, and general aloofness intrigued the other guests, but Lustig remained distant from the usual crowd of wealthy tourists, waiting for just the right sucker. It was not a lengthy wait.

Herman Loller, an arriviste who was anxious for acceptance, arrived at the hotel piloting a too-big, too-loud, and altogether horrifyingly ostentatious yacht. Lustig had his man. The boisterous newcomer delightedly accepted the Count's friendly overtures, for in those days a European title carried a lot of weight in higher American society. After only a brief acquaintance, the two men became regular dining companions.

As expected, it was not long before the boorish Loller was asking direct questions about how Lustig came to be so wealthy, but the Count remained evasive. The evasions served to make Loller's curiosity

Dream of fame. Lustig was a master at preying upon people who wanted a piece of the glamour of New York's Broadway and who had money to invest in dramatic productions. The only acting the suckers ever saw was Lustig passing himself off as a big-time producer.

even keener, until Lustig finally disclosed to his new confidant that he possessed a remarkable invention from the old country: a one-of-a-kind box devised by a deceased scientist that could perfectly reproduce any paper currency. As it was particularly effective with American thousand-dollar bills, Lustig explained, he would never have money worries again. Loller begged to see the box, so the Count invited him to his room for a demonstration.

In the suite, Lustig showed Loller an elegant wooden box with two slots and explained that inside were special chemicals that could duplicate any document perfectly; just roll the original through the top slot and roll a precut piece of blank treasury-grade paper in after it, and the chemicals did the rest. Lustig pulled a crisp thousand-dollar note from his wallet and placed it in the top slot of the box with the promise that an identical bill would emerge from the bottom slot after the six-hour process was complete. Lustig adjusted a few dials on the box and suggested that they dine and take drinks in the restaurant to fill the six hours.

When they returned, Lustig turned a roller and two wet but identical bills with identical serial numbers emerged from the bottom slot. Loller was astounded and, after checking each bill at separate banks for authenticity, offered forty-five thousand dollars for the invention. Lustig at last yielded for what he claimed were reasons of friendship and because he was sure he could make another box with the original specifications.

After the money changed hands, Lustig left Loller, who was excitedly putting another thousand-dollar bill in the money box. In the six hours it would take before Loller could learn he had been duped,

Lustig would travel far from Palm Beach. Long before Xerox was even a trademark, Lustig was successfully pedaling his "duplicating machines" to a small but amazed clientele. Of course, the process was bogus. Lustig's "duplicate" thousand-dollar bills passed a bank inspection because they were printed by the U.S. government; Lustig had simply altered the threes and eights in their serial numbers to give the appearance of an exact duplication. When he rolled the first bill into the box, it joined the "duplicate" that had been placed in the box before the sucker was given a demonstration.

An interesting note to the Loller story is that Loller never went to the police. He was so taken in by Lustig that when the money box inevitably failed to work for him as it had for the Count, Loller assumed there must be something he was doing wrong.

Lustig's Greatest Con

In 1922, Lustig found himself in Paris looking for a score when the papers offered him the opportunity for his most notorious scam. The Eiffel Tower, constructed in 1889 for the International Exposition, was in need of repair, and there was heated debate in government about the costs of repairing a structure that was never intended to be permanent. Rumors sifted through society that the landmark might even be disassembled. Lustig pounced.

From a rented room in the elegant Hotel Crillon, Lustig summoned the owners of France's largest iron-making companies to visit him in secret. The invitations were on official government stationery stolen specially for this purpose, and the industrialists were given authentic-looking credentials (forged, of course) identifying Lustig as a representative of the government. Lustig startled his guests with the news that the Eiffel Tower was indeed going to be demolished and that he was in charge of soliciting bids for the scrap iron that would have to be hauled off. Lustig explained that the political riskiness of such a move was his reason for meeting away from a government building, and he impressed upon these five powerful men the need for continued secrecy.

When the sealed bids arrived from each man a few days later, Lustig chose Andre Poisson's because the rags-to-riches industrialist had been the most impressed by Lustig's aristocratic airs and was, therefore, the best mark. Just before Poisson was to deliver the check—made out to "Cash" since there was still a need for secrecy—Lustig was forewarned by an accomplice that Poisson was somewhat suspicious about this late meeting to deliver the money being held in a place other than a government building. When Poisson arrived, Lustig hemmed and hawed, talking about the immensity of the deal they were negotiating and how it was a shame the government did not reward its servants with a commission of some sort. Poisson's suspicions were quickly erased—he got the hint that this bureaucrat was after a bribe! The secret meeting in the hotel room now made perfect sense to Poisson, who parted not only with a check for five million francs but a hefty cash bribe for Lustig as well.

Within hours, Lustig had cashed the check and fled to Eastern Europe expecting a huge uproar. For several days, Lustig scanned the French newspapers looking for the inevitable story of how Poisson

had been swindled, but the inevitable did not occur. When no story appeared, Lustig correctly calculated that Poisson had been too embarrassed to go public with his complaint, so the con artist boldly returned to Paris. He set up in the same hotel, contacted one of the other bidders about the scrap iron, and sold the Eiffel Tower again.

I'll throw in the Brooklyn Bridge for free. Many Parisians disliked the Eiffel Tower, which was originally intended only as a temporary structure for the 1889 International Exposition. Lustig used the doubt about the structure's future to score two big cons.

Loaded with cash, Lustig returned to the United States and continued his career of con artistry for decades more before the U.S. Secret Service finally put an end to his career. After eluding conviction on forty-seven previous arrests, the Count finally took the fall in 1935 on a counterfeiting charge and was sent to prison. He escaped custody once but was recaptured, and he died in prison in 1947.

One swindle too far. Two U.S. Secret Service Agents hold counterfeit money found in Lustig's possession in 1935. Lustig escaped custody but was recaptured and eventually died in an Oklahoma federal prison.

Lonely Hearts Scams

With sad eyes and a voice tragically close to breaking, Sigmund Engel's opening technique was to look deeply into the eyes of his carefully chosen victim, usually a widow to whom he had only just introduced himself. Engel would begin to say something, then pause and look sadly away. "What?" the widow would ask sympathetically. Perhaps she would touch Engel's arm with one of her elegantly jeweled hands. Engel would manage to look again into her eyes and answer, "You look

just like my wife…did." The effect was electrifying—such sincere grief on the face of the widower immediately gained sympathy from the woman who had not long been a widow herself.

Moving from town to town and combing the society pages and obituaries in search of future victims, Engel selected companions he knew had been widowed for only a few months and had inherited substantial fortunes. He would track his target and strike up an acquaintance with her, and soon the two would be married. Just a few days into the honeymoon, Engel would disappear with his new wife's cash, jewels, and heart. In a forty-nine-year career, Engel married two hundred women, from whom he bilked a total of six million dollars.

Engel's career ended in Chicago in 1949 after a woman he was pursuing, Genevieve Parro, recognized his tactics from something she had read in the papers. Parro led Engels on after she had alerted police, and he was finally arrested in a small shop buying luggage for their would-be honeymoon. At the police station, Resado Corrigan, whom he had fleeced for $8,700 (pretty small potatoes by his standards), shouted at the handcuffed Engels: "You beast! You took my money!" Engels suavely replied, "Madame, my apologies."

Engels used his savings to live as high as he could in prison, where he reportedly persuaded his jailers to escort him to Chicago's finest restaurants. But his time was running out. When Engel was put on trial, he declared that he had an evil twin brother who had done the evil deeds, but no one was convinced. The judge was not sympathetic and gave the con man a sentence of two to ten years.

Keeping Them Dangling

While Engel stalked and married his victims one at a time, his contemporary, Mildred Hill, was able to keep fifty men dangling at once with the mere promise of marriage. Hill operated through the mail by advertising in various newspapers around the country in search of a pen pal. Men who wrote to answer the ad were soon corresponding with an engaging writer whose prose was only exceeded by the

TOP: *Is it getting hot in here? Smooth operator Sigmund Engel is confronted by Pauline Langton, one of two hundred women he married and robbed. The ever-chivalrous Engel kissed her hand after she testified that he had stolen fifty thousand dollars in jewelry from her. After the romantic gesture, Langton exclaimed that she loved the old smoothie.*

BOTTOM: *Engel settles down with a Good Book and perhaps realizes that his courtroom defense hasn't got a prayer. Engel himself seemed amused when he claimed the charges against him were the work of his lunatic identical twin, "Arthur."*

strikingly beautiful photograph that came with the second or third letter.

It was not long before Mildred would let it drop that she was too poor to afford some trivial purchase, baiting the gentleman writer who would chivalrously volunteer money to help out. As the relationship developed by mail and occasionally by telephone, Mildred's mother might come to visit the suitor to check out his suitability for her daughter and

usually collect even more money. When the love-struck suitor had been touched for all the money and gifts that could be got, he received the sad news that pretty young Mildred had been wed to another. The suitor was left saddened and perhaps angry over a woman for whom he had such high hopes but whom he had never met face-to-face. Or had he?

At last, one of the jilted lovers suspected he had been conned and called the authorities, and Mildred Hill's scam was exposed for what it was. Although Hill had written the letters to hook the gents, she was not the pretty young thing in the photograph so many of them worshiped. The photo was a picture of Hill's daughter—it was Hill herself who met her correspondents in the role of the careful mother looking out for her daughter. The U.S. Postal Service shut down Mildred Hill, and she spent five years in prison for the thousands of dollars she had scammed through the mail.

Eternal telethon. Most of those moved to pledge money to PTL in hopes of salvation were people of middle to low income. The phones were always busy when Jim Bakker pronounced a financial crisis.

In the Name of the Father

If one were to see hell as Dante portrayed it, one might wonder why the Italian poet did not visualize a ring in the fiery underworld set aside specifically for those who would clean out a family's savings by manipulating their faith in God. Maybe the oversight was because Dante was Italian and all the best religio-hucksters have traditionally been American, from Aimee Semple MacPherson to the fictional Elmer Gantry to the master fleecer of the airwaves, Jim Bakker.

With his sincere voice and baby face, Jim Bakker emerged into the public eye in

How high was that pile of money? Jim Bakker's fingers were in all the pies at PTL and Heritage USA. His April Fools' Day bride, Tammy Faye, was usually alongside the preacher like a tearful Ed McMahon.

the 1960s as a devout man of God whose faith and earnest tears became effective money raisers in the early days of the Christian Broadcasting Network. Bakker's special gift was a thing called crisis fundraising. He would go on the air with a worried brow and begin describing the network's crushing debts, tears welling up in his eyes as he predicted the end of Christian broadcasting in America. By the time the tears had slid down his round cheeks and hit the studio floor, the switchboards would come boiling to life with true believers eager to pledge whatever they could to help the network and the boyish preacher out of their troubles.

In the early 1970s, Bakker started his own program, the PTL Club, and preached the theology of prosperity, quoting Luke 6:38, "Give that it may be given to you." Bakker joyously proclaimed the benefits that God rained upon those who gave generously to their churches and, more important, upon those who supported the ever-struggling-to-meet-the-monthly-bills PTL Club. Bakker modeled his show's format on Johnny Carson's *Tonight Show*, with his lachrymose wife, Tammy Faye, playing the role of Carson's sidekick, Ed McMahon.

By 1980, the show was a huge hit on Christian networks, and the Bakker lifestyle prospered just as Bakker's interpretation of the gospel said it should. The Bakkers kept two houses in California, one in Gatlinburg, Tennessee, and a condo in Florida, each worth upwards of $500,000. For local travel, three Mercedes worth $150,000 sparkled in the Bakker driveways. In addition to extravagant perquisites provided for the Bakkers by PTL, Jim Bakker received more than $4.7 million in salaries, bonuses, and retirement contributions from 1984 to 1987. Life, and seemingly the Lord, were being very good to Bakker, yet all of this opulence was evidently not quite enough. In the mid-1980s, PTL was becoming more than a TV show, and Jim Bakker was becoming something less than a forthright advocate of Jesus Christ.

Although the practices of many TV evangelists have raised the eyebrows of their critics, none of them has ever made the leap to big-time fraud on the scale of Jim Bakker and his cronies at PTL. In 1984, PTL offered its viewers a once-in-a-lifetime opportunity to purchase time-share lodging partnerships in a hotel to be the grand centerpiece of PTL's Disneylike Heritage USA complex. PTL offered twenty-five thousand lucky buyers an annual four-day stay in the Grand Hotel for the low price of one thousand dollars. The $25 million raised would, supposedly, build and maintain the hotel.

Sales were so good that PTL sold 66,683 of the twenty-five thousand partnerships they made available; in short, they were selling the same shares to different buyers. They made a second offering of thirty thousand partnerships in a second hotel, and again sold more than twice as many shares as they claimed were available. The total take from both scams was $158 million. Less than one-fourth of that went toward construction, no money was set aside for future upkeep, and no plan was made to accommodate the ninety thousand people who held partnerships but could never be lodged. More than $100 million vanished into the PTL operation, presumably into the hands of unscrupulous managers and Jim Bakker.

Bitter end. Bakker was disgraced when PTL's fraud was prosecuted. In a fit of anxiety and humiliation, Bakker once curled into a fetal ball and refused to come out from under a table.

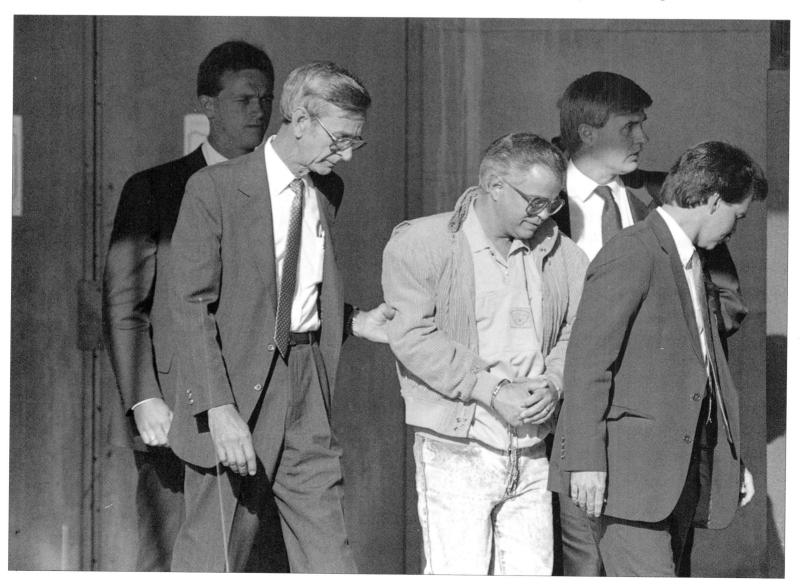

Traded for three hots and a cot. Conviction cost Bakker this extravagant parsonage in South Carolina (along with all his other houses), where he had boxes of fresh cinnamon rolls delivered every day because he liked the smell.

In 1987, it all collapsed for Bakker and PTL. Bakker began the year with an alleged seedy sex scandal involving church secretary Jessica Hahn, who PTL was forced to pay off with $265,000, and things just got worse. The feds descended on PTL, charging Bakker and PTL vice presidents Richard Dortch and David Taggart with fraud and malfeasance. The subsequent trial revealed that Bakker and his associates had fleeced more than fifty thousand believers out of more than $100 million under the most ruthless of pretenses—religious faith. All three men were sentenced to prison; Bakker himself was found guilty on twenty-four counts of fraud. "This man is a con man," proclaimed prosecuting United States Attorney Jerry Miller, "a common criminal." Miller was wrong about one thing: common criminals seldom score $100 million.

Must've Been Some Shower Curtain

Jet-plane rental for two-week holiday in California	$24,000
Houseboat decoration	$8,900
Swimming-pool waterslide	$8,500
Playhouse for kids with electricity and heat	$5,900
Shower curtain for daughter	$570

Jim and Tammy Faye Bakker's incidental expenses

An angry judge gave Bakker a forty-five-year sentence that was later commuted to fewer than ten. Tammy Faye Bakker, whom Jim had married on April Fools' Day 1961, divorced her husband in 1993 after a failed attempt to start her own religious program out of a Florida strip mall. Bakker was successful in prison, conducting a program to help fellow inmates give up smoking. Bakker, free after seven years, continues to proclaim his faith in God and wants to preach again in a small church. The victims of the PTL scam will never see their money again.

Peter-to-Paul Scams

One component of the American dream—certainly on par with universal suffrage, individual liberty, and owning a home of one's own—is the notion that anybody has a shot at getting very, very rich. At the turn of the century, everyone in the United States was looking for fat payoffs in the boom-bust cycles that had characterized the American economy for decades. With the likes of Vanderbilt, Gould,

surefire plan for mass investment that he claimed would one day control the stock market. An artistic reproduction of old Ben Franklin smiled down from the wall at the first persons intrepid enough to come to Miller's office and invest a few dollars. When they returned a week later, sure enough, the investors were paid—in cash—a 10 percent dividend on their initial investment.

The promise of a 520 percent annual return paid out weekly probably did set off "too good to be true" alarms in most people, but as the initial investors continued to get their weekly cash dividends, other would-be Rockefellers came running. In just a few weeks the word spread,

Ponzi

Charles Ponzi started a scam in 1920 similar to the Franklin Syndicate. Ponzi promised huge earnings by trading in international postage coupons. In this Peter-to-Paul scam, Ponzi claimed he was buying postage coupons in foreign countries and exchanging them in countries where they were more valuable. No coupons were ever purchased, however, and Ponzi lived flamboyantly on the ten million dollars his scheme brought in—until the government closed him down. Ponzi's flashy ways and notoriety have led some to call the Peter-to-Paul scam a "Ponzi Scheme," even though he did not originate the fraud.

Rockefeller, and Morgan getting rich quick, many common citizens thought and hoped the same might happen to them. The appearance of the Benjamin Franklin Syndicate seemed an answer to the common man's prayers.

Former Wall Street clerk William Franklin Miller lived in one of New York's hardworking, frugal German neighborhoods when he created the Franklin Syndicate in 1899. Promising a 10 percent *weekly* return on investments of any size, Miller attracted his first few investors with vague allusions to his contacts on Wall Street (he had none) and a purported

and the modest Franklin Syndicate offices were flooded with new investors anxious to put down their hard-earned dollars. There were so many people clamoring to get in that the front stairway of the building collapsed under their combined weight. People anxiously queued up in lines that literally circled the block around the small office building.

When investors finally got inside, they found an office cleverly set up to encourage their confidence. As each new investor laid his money on the desk, he could look through a glass partition into the other half of the office, where earlier investors were picking up their weekly dividend. Clearly, Miller's investment scheme must be working. The only thing wrong with this prosperous picture was that the funds were never actually invested. Miller was simply circulating the money from new investors to old investors—robbing Peter to pay Paul—and skimming a healthy bit of cash right off the top for himself. As long as new investors kept lining up, no one would know what was going on. The scam was made even easier because a great deal of what he paid out to the suckers was immediately plowed right back into the syndicate by the suckers themselves in hopes of even greater returns.

For two years, the Franklin Syndicate took in an estimated eighty thousand dollars a day without investing a dime in any stock or bond. Even when the government and reputable investment journals began publicly warning citizens about the Franklin Syndicate, investors refused to believe the truth. Not until Miller absconded to Canada with two million in cash did the syndicate collapse. Thousands of investors, mostly working people, were left with nothing.

Upon fleeing the country, Miller left $170,000 with his notoriously crooked lawyer, Robert Adams Ammon, with instructions that the money be used to take care of his family. But the rip-off artist was in turn ripped off by his attorney, who meted out a paltry five dollars a week to Miller's wife and children. But Miller would have his revenge.

Unhappy to be living away from his home and family, or maybe just afraid of being extradited, Miller returned to the United States to face charges and was ultimately sentenced to ten years in prison.

After serving only a few years and with more than a shadow of irony, however, Miller was pardoned in 1905 in exchange for testifying against his former attorney in the trial that sent Ammon to jail. Most of the money with which Miller fled— money earned by the hard labor of others—was never recovered.

Home-Stake: World's Biggest Scam

The biggest Peter-to-Paul scam ever was run out of Oklahoma, but the primary rubes were not country people. Robert Trippet stung the biggest names from America's two biggest cities for an estimated $100 million, which he so craftily disseminated that lawyers and accountants still can't say exactly where all of the money went.

Trippet, a Tulsa attorney, was a successful man and a pillar of his community when he started the Home-Stake Production Company in the 1950s. He took the company public in 1964 and marketed shares in oil-drilling ventures as a tax shelter for the rich, who would either turn a nifty profit if Home-Stake hit oil or have a substantial tax write-off if they drilled a dry hole. Trippet started off fairly legitimately as he slowly built a stable of investors, always with an eye toward hooking people who possessed big money. Over the years it seemed that high-rolling, well-connected shareholders did much better than the more average Joes when it came to dividend payments from Home-Stake.

Trippet's big entry into the moneyed classes came when several executives from General Electric invested money in Home-Stake. Like the Franklin Syndicate

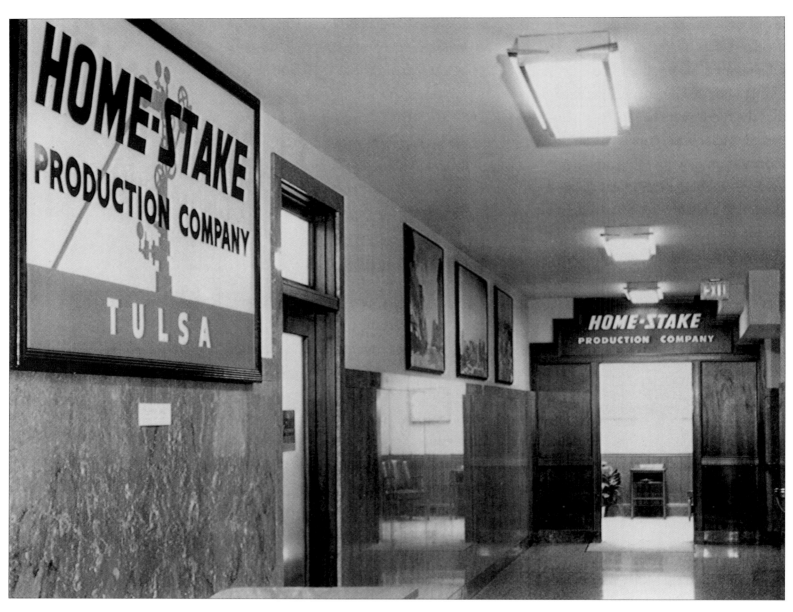

After the fall. The Home-Stake Production Company's offices in Tulsa were quiet after Feds closed them down, but questions remain regarding where the bulk of the money went.

and Charles Ponzi before him, Trippet made sure that these important men got high returns on their investments. Unlike Ponzi and Miller, however, Trippet did not promise or deliver returns that were so astronomical that they would set off the "too good to be true" alarms in the minds of these sophisticated captains of business. Favorable word soon spread, and Trippet started getting telephone calls from East and West Coast investment advisers, whom Trippet also sized up carefully.

Although many of the investment counselors made honest errors, Trippet cultivated the less-than-honest moneymen with high yields and loans that would never be repaid. Now a lot of people with

deep pockets were talking about Home-Stake, and the fleecing of the suckers could begin in earnest.

From the late 1960s until 1974, more than $140 million flowed into Trippet's Tulsa coffers from an impressive array of famous and important people. Jack Benny, Candice Bergen, Barbra Streisand, Senators Jacob Javits and Ernest Hollings, the eminent financial writer George J.W. Goodman, and Dean Witter, Jr., are just a few of the people who cut checks for Home-Stake Production Company. If any of these pigeons or their representatives came to have a look into what Home-Stake was up to, Trippet would happily show them two shallow wells he had drilled in Santa Maria, California (where, of course, there was no oil), and an impressive array of pipeline through which the oil supposedly flowed off to the market (the pipes were farm irrigation equipment painted to look like oil pipeline). The bogus wells and fake pipeline fooled many, including actor Elliott Gould and General Electric executive Fred Borch.

In 1974, the Securities and Exchange Commission and the Internal Revenue Service finally caught up with Trippet, who had to close down Home-Stake. The books showed that in the last five years of Home-Stake's operation, from 1969 to 1974, Home-Stake had taken in $120 million, of which only $3 million was spent on oil exploration. Only $20 million had been paid back to investors as dividends. The rest, nearly $100 million, had been moved so cleverly through phantom accounts and offshore banks that even the IRS was at a loss to track down more than a fraction of it. Out of all that money, Federal agents could only nail Trippet on an illegal transfer of $3 million from Home-Stake to his personal account; they had to accept a settlement of $3.7 million on a tax claim of $35 million. Where the rest of the money went, nobody knows.

The movie stars, business executives, and other big shots had to eat their losses and settle for being footnotes in the greatest Peter-to-Paul scam of all time.

Home-Stake's Famous Hoaxees

Alan Alda
Jack Benny
Candice Bergen
Jacqueline Bisset
Bill Blass
Joseph Bologna
Diahann Carroll
David Cassidy
Jack Cassidy
Oleg Cassini
Tony Curtis
Sandy Dennis
Phyllis Diller
Faye Dunaway
Bob Dylan
Mia Farrow
Elliott Gould
Buddy Hackett
Ernest Hollings
Jacob Javits
Shirley Jones
Walter Matthau
Liza Minnelli
Mike Nichols
Buffy Sainte-Marie
Barbara Walters
Dean Witter, Jr.

The man who knows. Robert Trippett, a seemingly respectable lawyer and businessman, got his start as a crook by smuggling cigarettes from out of state into Oklahoma to sell without paying tax. The Securities and Exchange Commission never ran down all the millions Trippett bounced through offshore banks.

Bibliography

Abadinsky, Howard. *The Criminal Elite*. Westport, Conn.: Greenwood Press, 1983.

Baker, Albie. *Stolen Sweets*. New York: Saturday Review Press, 1973.

Barrell, Clyde, and Brian Cashinellar. *Crime in Britain Today*. London: Broadway House, 1975.

Behn, Noel. *Big Stick-Up at Brinks*. New York: Putnam, 1977.

Delano, Anthony. *Slip-Up: Fleet Street, Scotland Yard and the Great Train Robbery*. New York: Quadrangle/The New York Times Book Co., 1975.

Esterow, Milton. *The Art Stealers*. New York: Macmillan Publishing, 1973.

Follett, Ken, and Rene Louis Maurice. *The Gentlemen of 16 July*. New York: Pinnacle Books, 1978.

Gunther, Max. *D.B. Cooper: What Really Happened*. Chicago: Contemporary Books, 1985.

Haywood, Ian. *Faking It*. New York: St. Martin's Press, 1987.

Hinton, Ted, and Larry Grove. *Ambush: The Real Story of Bonnie and Clyde*. Bryan, Tex.: Shoal Creek Publishing, 1979.

Jeffers, H. Paul. *Bloody Business: An Anecdotal History of Scotland Yard*. New York: Pharos Books, 1992.

Keating, Tom, with Frank Norman and Geraldine Norman. *The Fake's Progress*. London: Hutchinson and Co., 1977.

Kilbracken, Lord. *Van Meegeren: Master Art Forger*. New York: Charles Scribner's Sons, 1967.

McClintick, David. *Stealing From the Rich*. New York: Quill, 1983.

McLeave, Hugh. *Rogues in the Gallery*. Boston: D.R. Godine, 1981.

Moffit, Donald. *Swindled*. Princeton, N. J.: Dow Jones Books, 1976.

Nash, Jay Robert. *Hustlers and Con-Men*. New York: M. Evans & Co. Inc., 1976.

Patterson, Richard. *The Train Robbery Era*. Boulder, Colo.: Pruett Publishing, 1991.

Pileggi, Nicholas. *Wiseguy: Life in a Mafia Family*. New York: Simon & Schuster, 1985.

Reit, Seymour. *The Day They Stole the Mona Lisa*. New York: Summit Books, 1981.

Rose, Colin. *The World's Greatest Ripoffs*. New York: Sterling Publishing, 1978.

Rossberg, Robert R. *Game of Thieves*. New York: Everest House, 1981.

Rhodes, Bernie. *D.B. Cooper...The Real McCoy*. Salt Lake City: University of Utah Press, 1991.

Saint-Germain, Comte de (Edgar Valcourt-Vermont). *The Dalton Brothers and Their Astounding Career of Crime*. New York: F. Fell, 1954.

Tidwell, Gary. *Anatomy of a Fraud: Inside the Finances of the PTL Ministeries*. New York: John Wiley and Sons Inc., 1993.

Toland, John. *The Dillinger Days*. New York: Random House, 1963.

Photography Credits

Index